THE DIVIN

NOTES

including
- *General Introduction*
- *Introduction to* Paradiso
- *Synopsis*
- *Summaries and Commentaries*
- *List of Characters*
- *Review Questions and Study Projects*
- *Selected Bibliography*

by
Harold M. Priest, Ph.D.
Department of English
University of Denver

Cliffs Notes
INCORPORATED
LINCOLN, NEBRASKA 68501

Editor	Consulting Editor
Gary Carey, M.A. University of Colorado	James L. Roberts, Ph.D. Department of English University of Nebraska

ISBN 0-8220-0396-1
© Copyright 1972
by
Cliffs Notes, Inc.
All Rights Reserved
Printed in U.S.A.

1995 Printing

Cliffs Notes, Inc.   Lincoln, Nebraska

CONTENTS

General Introduction

The story of the *Divine Comedy* is simple: one day Dante finds himself lost in a dark wood; but Virgil appears, rescues him from that savage place, and guides him to a contemplation of Hell and Purgatory. Then, having confessed his faults, and with Beatrice as his guide, he is conducted into Paradise and attains a glimpse of the face of God.

Dante gave the title of *Comedy* to his masterpiece because the word indicated a pleasant or (as Dante himself put it) a "prosperous" ending after a "horrible" beginning. Dante used the humble lowly language "which even women can understand," rather than the sublime language of tragedy. The adjective "divine" was added to the title later, apparently by an editor some time in the sixteenth century.

The *Divine Comedy* is distinctly a product of medieval times. Its view of the universe is the Ptolemaic view; its social setting that of the jealous, warring city-states of Italy, and of the powerful, arrogant, and feuding aristocrats and the political factions which supported them. Over all were the contesting powers of a fading empire and a grasping papacy.

In attempting understanding, one may become so entangled in the complexities of the *Comedy* and its environment that one loses sight of Dante the man. And it was Dante, the man of his times, who wrote the *Divine Comedy* – a man whose lifelong devotion to the figure of Beatrice was in the highest tradition of courtly love; whose political feuds were first with the party of the opposition, then with factions within his own party, until he formed a party of his own; a man who believed firmly in alchemy and astrology, in witchcraft and spells; and finally, an intensely human man, with fierce hatreds and loyalties, with no little vanity, with pity, and with love.

The date of the composition of the *Divine Comedy* is uncertain, but undoubtedly the poem was written during Dante's exile. Even here there is some disagreement, for there is a tradition which insists that the first seven cantos were written before he was banished from Florence. The predominant opinion is that it was begun around 1307; the setting of the poem is the year 1300. There is some evidence that the *Inferno* had been completed and circulated before 1314, and that the *Purgatorio* followed very soon after. The *Paradiso* was completed shortly before Dante's death in 1321 and released posthumously by his sons.

The *Divine Comedy* is a monumental work of imagination, dedicated in spirit to an immortal love; it is mortal to the point of repugnance in its beginning, mystical almost beyond understanding at its close.

DANTE'S LIFE

Dante Alighieri was born in Florence in May, 1265, of an old family, of noble origin but no longer wealthy. His education was probably typical of any youth of his time and station: he studied the *trivium* and *quadrivium,* probably spent a year, or part of a year, at the University of Bologna, and came under the influence of some of the learned men of his day. Most notable of these was Ser Brunetto Latini, whose influence Dante records in his poem (*Inferno* 15).

In accordance with custom, Dante was betrothed in his youth to Gemma Donati, daughter of Manetto Donati. These betrothals and marriages were matters of family alliance, and Gemma's dowry was fixed as early as 1277, when Dante was twelve years old. There were at least three children: sons Pietro and Jacopo, and a daughter Antonia, who later entered a convent at Ravenna and took the name of Sister Beatrice. A third son, Giovanni, is sometimes mentioned.

There can be no doubt that the great love of Dante's life, and the greatest single influence on his work, was his beloved Beatrice. He first met her when he was nine years old and she was eight. The meeting took place in her father's home, probably at a May Day festival. Dante has described this meeting in his *Vita Nuova*. He tells of seeing the child Beatrice, wearing a crimson gown and looking like an angel. From that day on, his life and work was dedicated to her. He mentions no other meeting with her until nine years later, when he saw her on the street, dressed in white, accompanied by two other girls. She greeted him sweetly by name, and he was in raptures. A short time later, having heard gossip linking his name with another young woman, she passed him without speaking, and Dante mourned for days, determining to mend his ways.

If all this seems slightly preposterous, it is necessary to remember two things: that the young women of marriageable age were so strictly chaperoned that it was virtually impossible to have even a speaking acquaintance with them and that Dante's love for Beatrice was in the strictest tradition of courtly love, wherein the lover addressed his beloved as being completely out of his reach, and which viewed marriage between the lovers as impossible, in fact undesirable.

To what extent this was, at first, a true and lasting love cannot be determined. There is little doubt that Dante enjoyed the sweet misery of his situation and the sympathy of other ladies for his plight. After the death of Beatrice, and particularly after his exile, he put away his adolescent fancies, and Beatrice became a true inspiration.

Beatrice was married in about 1287 to Simone de' Bardi, a wealthy banker of Florence, a marriage of alliance of the two houses and one completely immaterial to Dante and his work.

Dante wrote many poems in praise of his lady during her lifetime, and when she died in 1290, at the age of twenty-five, he was inconsolable. He had had a dream of her death, and in her honor collected the poems he had written about her, which are included in the *Vita Nuova*. The later *Comedy* was also inspired by her memory.

Dante's public life began in 1289, when he fought against Arezzo at Campaldino. In 1295 he was one of the council for the election of the priors of Florence, and in May, 1300, went as ambassador to San Gemignano to invite that commune to an assembly of the Guelph cities of Tuscany. From June 15 to August of the same year, he was one of the priors of Florence, and it was during that year that his best friend, Guido Cavalcanti (*Inferno*, Canto 22), caused a street riot on May Day. Guido was exiled to Sarzana by the officers of the city, one of whom was Dante. Sarzana proved so unhealthful that Guido petitioned to return to Florence, and was allowed to do so. He died of malaria, contracted in Sarzana, in August, 1300.

Dante was vigorously opposed to the interference of the pope in secular affairs, and was induced to take a stand with the Whites when the Blacks favored the intrigues of the pope. Charles of Valois was coming to Florence, ostensibly as a peacemaker between the two factions but in reality as a partisan of the Blacks and supporter of the pope. In October, 1301, Dante and two other men were chosen as ambassadors on a mission to Rome, rightly suspecting the motives of Charles as peacemaker. After they had left Florence, the Blacks easily took over control of the city with the help of Charles, and Dante was exiled from his native city, never to return.

The terms of exile were harsh: Dante was charged with graft, with intrigue against the peace of the city, and with hostility against the pope, among other things. The list of charges is so long that it is reminiscent of those brought against the political enemies of any party in power today. In addition, a heavy fine was imposed, and Dante was forbidden to hold public office in Florence for the rest of his life.

Dante did not appear to answer the charges — it probably would not have been safe to do so — and a heavier penalty was imposed: in addition to confiscation of his property, he was sentenced to be burnt alive if caught. Also, his sons, when they reached their legal majority at age fourteen, were compelled to join him in exile.

Thus began Dante's wanderings. At first he joined in the political intrigues of his fellow exiles, but, disgusted by what he considered their wickedness and stupidity, he formed a party by himself. It is not known exactly where he spent the years of his exile, though part of the time he was with the Malaspini, and he also spent time at the court of Can Grande della Scala in Verona, with whom he remained on good terms for the rest of his life.

Once during the years of his banishment his hopes for peace in Italy, and his own return to Florence, were revived. This was in the reign of Henry VII of Luxemburg, who announced his intention of coming to Italy to be crowned. Dante addressed a letter to his fellow citizens urging them to welcome Henry as emperor. When Henry was met by strong opposition, Dante in great bitterness sent a letter to him, urging him to put down the rebellion quickly; he also addressed a letter in similar vein to Florence, using abusive terms which could not be forgiven. When Henry's expedition failed, and the hopes of empire died with him, Dante was not included in the amnesty granted certain exiles. Later, amnesty was extended to him on the condition that he admit his guilt and ask forgiveness publicly, which the poet refused to do. His sentence of death was renewed.

Dante's last years were spent in Ravenna, under the protection of Guido Novello da Polenta. They seem to have been years of relative contentment in compatible company — but Ravenna was not Florence. One final mission was entrusted to Dante: he was sent to Venice in the summer of 1321 by his patron in an unsuccessful attempt to avert a war between Ravenna and Venice. On his return trip, he fell ill, possibly of malaria. He reached Ravenna and died there on the night of September 13, 1321.

He was buried with the honors due him. Several times during the following centuries, the city of Florence sought to have his body interred with honor in the place of his birth, but even the intercession of popes could not bring this about. His opinion of the citizens of his city was clearly stated in the full title of his great work: *The Comedy of Dante Alighieri, Florentine by Citizenship, Not by Morals.*

Dante still lies in the monastery of the Franciscan friars in Ravenna.

DANTE'S WORLD

Dante's world was threefold: the world of politics, the world of theology, and the world of learning. His *Comedy* encompasses and builds upon all of these, and so interdependent were they that it would be impossible to say that any one was the most important.

Throughout the Middle Ages, politics was dominated by the struggle between the two greatest powers of that age: the papacy and the empire. Each believed itself to be of divine origin and to be indispensable to the welfare of mankind. The cause of this struggle was the papal claim to temporal power, supported and justified by the spurious "Donation of Constantine." This document, which was a forgery of the eighth century, maintained that Emperor Constantine, before leaving for Byzantium, had transferred to the Bishop of Rome, Pope Sylvester I, political dominion over Italy and the western empire.

Dante lived in an era of virtually autonomous communes, ruled by either an autocratic hereditary count or a council elected from an aristocratic—and exclusive—few. The political situation was never stable, and the vendettas went on forever, family against family, party against party, city against city.

The strife began in the tenth century with Otto I, the emperor who laid the foundation for the power which was to transform Germany into the mightiest state in Europe and who dreamed of restoring the Holy Roman Empire. At the beginning of the eleventh century, the situation worsened, with Henry IV humiliated at Canossa by an aggressive opponent, autocratic Pope Gregory VII (Hildebrand).

In the first part of the thirteenth century, the growing conflict was headed by two outstanding antagonists: Innocent III, the most powerful of all the popes, and the brilliant Frederick II, King of Germany, Emperor of Rome, and King of Naples and Sicily, the most gifted of all the monarchs of the Middle Ages. The enmity of the pope, who was firmly resolved to free Italy from German authority, shook the stability of the empire, which was already undermined by the insubordination of the princes in Germany and the rebellion of some of the city-states of northern Italy.

When Frederick died in 1250, he left a very unstable situation to be handled by his successors, especially in Italy. There, in 1266, his illegitimate son Manfred was defeated and killed in the battle fought at Benevento against Charles of Anjou, who had been summoned to Italy by the pope. Two years later, this same Charles defeated Corradino, Frederick's grandson, at Tagliacozzo, and put him to death. Thus the line of the descendants of the great emperor was extinguished, and Italy was lost to the empire.

In reading Dante, indeed throughout medieval history, one hears much about two major political factions, the Guelphs and the Ghibellines. In Italy the party lines were originally drawn over the dispute between the papacy and the emperor for temporal authority. The Ghibellines, representing the feudal aristocracy, wished to retain the power of the emperor in Italy as well as in Germany. The Guelphs were mainly supported by the rising middle-class merchant society, who hoped to rid Italy of foreign influence and maintain the control of governments in their independent communes. They espoused the cause of the papacy in opposition to the emperor.

The rivalry between the two parties not only set one city against another but also divided the same city and the same family into factions. In time the original alliances and allegiances became confused in strange ways. For example, Dante, who was a Guelph, was a passionate supporter of imperial authority all his life.

In Florence the Guelphs and Ghibellines succeeded each other, alternately ruling the city. During the rein of Frederick II, the Ghibellines, supported by the emperor, gained the upper hand and drove the Guelphs out of the city. But at the death of Frederick II, in 1250, the

Guelphs were recalled to Florence for a temporary reconciliation and later gained control of the city.

The Ghibellines again returned to power in 1260, and ruled the city until 1266, but the next year the Guelphs, aided by French forces, gained supremacy in the city, and the Ghibellines left Florence, never to return.

Dante was an ardent White Guelph, putting his hopes for Italy's future in the restoration of the empire, and to the end of his days was politically active, though ultimately he was forced by the violence of his views to form a party "by himself," and, as a White, was actually allied to the Ghibellines.

Not even the supremacy of the Guelphs, however, endowed Florence with a peaceful and stable government, for in 1300 the Guelph party split into two factions: the Whites and the Blacks, led respectively by the families of the Cerchi and the Donati. The basis of this split was the usual blood-feud between two families. In nearby Pistoia, a family quarrel existed between two branches of the Cancellieri family. The first wife of the original Cancelliere was named Bianca, and her descendants called themselves Whites in her honor. The name of the second wife is not known, but her descendants, in opposition to the Whites, called themselves Blacks. The quarrel erupted into open violence after a murder committed by one Foccaccia (mentioned by Dante in Canto 32 of the *Inferno*).

The Guelphs of Florence, in the interests of maintaining the precarious peace of the district, intervened in the hostilities, and in so doing furthered the jealous rivalry of the Cerchi and the Donati families, who naturally took opposite sides. The city was torn by strife; personal ambitions, feuds, and the arrogance of individuals and families further agitated the situation.

At this point, the Blacks secretly enlisted the aid of Pope Boniface VIII, who intervened in the affairs of the city, largely in his own interest. The pope considered the throne of the empire still vacant, since Albert I had not received his crown in Rome. In his assumed capacity as vicar of the emperor, Boniface plotted to extend the rule of the church over the territory of Tuscany. To accomplish this, he first obtained the favor of the Blacks, then dispatched Charles of Valois, brother of the King of France, to Florence, ostensibly as a peacemaker, but actually as a supporter of the Blacks. In 1302, with the help of Charles of Valois, the Blacks gained control of the city. In the list of some six hundred Whites banished from Florence was the name of the citizen Dante Alighieri.

While the rest of Italy, like Florence, was troubled by rivalries between parties, or by wars of city against city, in Germany the emperor's throne was vacant, first because of an interregnum, then because of a conflict between two rival claimants. The emperor's position was still regarded as vacant by the Italians when the two emperors who followed, Rudolph of Hapsburg and Albert I, failed to come to Italy to be crowned and paid no attention to Italian affairs. Therefore when the news came that Henry of Luxemburg, who succeeded Albert I in 1308, was coming to Italy to oppose King Robert of Sicily, many Italians, for whom Dante was the most eloquent and fervent spokesman, welcomed the prospect with feverish enthusiasm. They saw in the figure of Henry the end of all the woes which had wracked the peninsula.

Henry was crowned at Milan early in 1311. Very soon after, he faced the armed hostility of the opposing party, which had Florence as its leader. Henry, nevertheless, was able to reach Rome and be crowned there in 1312. The coronation took place in the church of St. John Lateran rather than in St. Peter's because the latter was being held by the forces of King Robert of Sicily. The emperor was still fighting to unite the empire when he died in the summer of 1313, succumbing to a fever with suspicious suddenness. The death of Henry put an end forever to the expectations of Dante and all other Italians who had longed for the restoration of the imperial power in Italy.

Dante's theological ideas were strictly orthodox, that is, those of medieval Catholicism. He accepted church dogma without reservation. His best authorities for insight into the more complex problems confronting the medieval thinkers were Augustine, Albertus Magnus, and Thomas Aquinas. He followed the Pauline doctrine of predestination and grace as presented by Augustine, but he managed to bring this into a kind of conformity with free will, to which he firmly adhered. Man has inherited sin and death through Adam's fall, but also hope of salvation through Christ's redemption. God in his love created humans with the power of perceiving good and evil and the opportunity of choosing. On the basis of their choice depended their eternal bliss or damnation. Those who set their will against the divine law were sentenced to Inferno and everlasting torment. Those who sinned but confessed and repented were given their reward in heaven after a period of purifying atonement in Purgatory. Thus repentance, the acceptance of divine law, was the crux of judgment in the afterlife.

Among the familiar tenets of medieval theology, we recognize such concepts as the "seven deadly sins" in Purgatory and the corresponding seven virtues in Paradise. The doctrine that only those persons who had been baptized as worshipers of Christ were to be admitted to Paradise is expressed in the treatment of the souls in Limbo (*Inferno* 4). Of the many more complex theological concepts expounded through the *Commedia*, explanations will be offered in the textual commentaries.

In castigating the individual popes (and particularly his bitter enemy, Boniface VIII), he was in no way showing disrespect for the *office* of the papacy, for which he held the greatest reverence. He was, in fact, following the long tradition of critics, many of them in high places in the church, who had not hesitated to recall popes to the duties and responsibilities of the chair of Peter. Dante held to the ideal of the papacy and the empire as the dual guardians of the welfare of man, spiritual and secular, each deriving its separate powers directly from God.

Readers cannot fail to recognize Dante's erudition. He appears to have taken all learning for his province, or what passed for learning then. The fact that much of the scientific teaching was hopelessly in error is not Dante's responsibility. The fact that he displayed extraordinary curiosity and avid interest in all branches of scientific learning (geography, geology, astronomy, astrology, natural history, and optics) reveals something important about the poet's mind.

Among the concepts that influenced the plan of the *Commedia* was the belief that only the northern hemisphere of the earth was inhabited, that the southern hemisphere was covered with water except for the mount of Purgatory. The scheme of the heavens was dictated by the Ptolemaic, or geocentric, system of astronomy, upon which Dante based the entire plan of *Paradiso*.

In addition to his thorough and easy familiarity with the Bible, Dante displays a scholar's acquaintance with not only those great theologians previously mentioned (Augustine, Aquinas, etc.) but with a score of others.

Finally, wide reading and absorption of works of *belles lettres,* especially the Latin classics, was of the greatest importance. (Further details will be given later in the discussion of sources of the *Comedy.*)

DANTE'S MINOR WORKS

LA VITA NUOVA

The *Vita Nuova (New Life)* is a little book consisting of the love poems written in honor of Beatrice from 1283 to 1292. Written in Italian ("the Vulgar Tongue"), they were collected and linked by a commentary in prose, probably in 1292.

The book of memories and confessions presents a proper introduction to the *Divine Comedy*, as it speaks of a love which, in the mature life, through the path of philosophy and the ascendancy of faith, led the poet to his greatest poetical achievement. However, in the *Vita Nuova* the inspiration comes, without doubt, from reality. Beatrice is not an allegorical creature, but a real woman, smiling, weeping, walking in the street, and praying in the church. From the sincerity of its inspiration, the book derives a note of freshness and originality that is remarkable for that age.

The poems, most of them sonnets and canzoni, are arranged in a carefully planned pattern. These lyrics, like all of Dante's early verses, show the influence of the new school in Bologna, led by Guido Guinizelli, which was identified as *il dolce stil nuovo* (the sweet new style). This group of poets followed the tradition of the poetry of courtly love in certain respects, but developed techniques of greater refinement than their predecessors and treated love in a lofty, spiritual vein.

The prose passages accompanying each poem include not only an account of the circumstances which suggested the writing of the poem but also some analysis of the techniques employed in the construction of the poem, thus giving a unique character to the work.

CANZONIERE

Canzoniere, also in Italian, comprises the collected lyrics other than those included in the *Vita Nuova* and the *Convivio*. Love poems predominate in the collection, some to Beatrice, some to other ladies. The volume includes a group of poems called the "Pietra" lyrics because they were dedicated to a woman "hard as stone." These poems reveal a violent and sensual passion but demonstrate as well experiments in very complicated artistic techniques. There are also exchanges of poems between Dante and other poets, sometimes complimentary and sometimes caustic and satirical. Other poems in the collection, written during exile, deal with moral and civic doctrine.

IL CONVIVIO

The *Convivio* (the *Banquet*) was written during the exile, possibly in the years 1306-07. The name is metaphorical. Dante means to prepare a banquet of learning and science for such people as princes, barons, knights, and women, who are too busy with civil and social affairs to attend schools and familiarize themselves with scholarship. Such being the aim of the work, Dante employs the vernacular, the common speech, which will benefit a greater number of people, in spite of the fact that in those days Latin was generally required for a learned and scholastic commentary.

According to his original plan, the work was to consist of fourteen chapters, each with a *canzone* and an elaborate prose commentary. Actually only four sections were written, one being the introduction and each of the other three presenting a *canzone* with its commentary.

The two ideas of greatest importance discussed in the *Convivio* are the nobility and the empire. Speaking of the first, Dante maintains that true nobility does not derive from heredity or from the possession of wealth but rather from the practice of virtue. The ideas about the empire, of which Dante here speaks only briefly, were further developed in the *De Monarchia* and in the *Divine Comedy*. However, the secular office of the empire is already seen in the perspective of a divine plan ordained by God for the redemption of man and his betterment in the earthly life.

DE VULGARI ELOQUENTIA

After demonstrating the efficacy of the vernacular in the *Convivio*, Dante made it the subject of a treatise which, being addressed to scholarly people, was written in Latin. The treatise was to consist of four books, but only the first book and sixteen chapters of the second were completed.

The work deals with the origin and the history of languages in general, then attempts a classification of the Italian dialects. The ideal language is considered to be the "illustrious, vulgar tongue," a common language for the whole peninsula which would combine the best qualities of the different dialects. To Dante, this ideal seemed to have been attained by the writers of the Sicilian school, and the poets of "the sweet new style" *(il dolce stil nuovo).*

EPISTLES

All of the *Epistles* were written in Latin, and among the thirteen left to us (one of which may be a forgery), the three written to Henry VII on the occasion of his coming to Italy show the same spirit of prophecy which inspires some of the more eloquent passages of the *Divine Comedy.* Dante strongly desired the unification of Italy under Henry's rule and a peaceful Florence to which he could return from exile.

One of the most interesting is that addressed to the six Italian cardinals after the death of Pope Clement V at Avignon. It exhorts the cardinals to elect an Italian pope who will restore the Holy See to Rome. In this letter, as in the *De Monarchia* and the *Divine Comedy,* political and religious problems are closely related. Dante desires not only the return of the popes to Rome but also their peaceful cooperation with the emperors and the moral reformation of the church, then corrupted by simony and avarice.

His letter to Can Grande della Scala outlining the purpose and ideas of the *Comedy* gives the four levels of its interpretation, and serves as an introduction to the work. This letter accompanied some cantos of the *Paradiso,* which Dante dedicated to Can Grande. Boccaccio, in his biography of Dante, relates that the poet was in the habit of writing several cantos of his work, then sending them to Can Grande, his friend and patron.

DE MONARCHIA

The *De Monarchia* states in the most complete manner Dante's views upon the perfect government of human society. Being of universal interest, it was written in Latin, probably during the time Henry was en route to Italy. It was meant to be a warning to the numerous opponents encountered by the emperor on his way to Rome.

Divided into three parts, the book maintains that the empire is necessary for the welfare of mankind because it is the only means of establishing peace in the world; that the right to exercise this office belongs to the Roman people; that the authority of the emperor, like that of the pope, comes directly from God. Thence derives the independence of the empire from the church because both powers are autonomous and destined to guide mankind, respectively, toward earthly happiness and toward celestial beatitude; the emperor, however, should show the pope the same kind of reverence that a son should show his father.

Dante was convinced that the principal cause of the evils devastating Italy and the world was to be found in the pope's usurpation of the authority assigned by God to the emperor. He was particularly opposed to the policies of Boniface VIII, and strongly condemned the spurious "Donation of Constantine," which was claimed as the authorization of the pope's temporal power.

The claim that Rome should be the seat of the emperor did not conflict with its being the seat of papal authority as well, since the two powers have to coordinate their plans for the welfare of mankind. The emperor, Dante believed, could not be universally recognized as such unless he was crowned by the pope in Rome. In other words, Italy, with Rome as the seat of the empire and of the papacy, had been ordained by God to give the world a universal spiritual and temporal government.

THE DIVINE COMEDY

SOURCES OF THE *COMEDY*

Dante used two main literary sources in the writing of his *Comedy:* The religious and theological works of earlier times, and the classics.

It is evident, of course, that he drew heavily upon the Vulgate Bible, and he refers to it as one thoroughly familiar with it. Probably next in importance, to him, were the writings of St. Thomas Aquinas, and, to a lesser degree, those of other saints and religious philosophers.

The Latin classics had been an important part of Dante's formal training and certainly of his later reading. His eloquence in Latin is evident in his own writing to the end of his life. The study of philosophy, particularly the work of Aristotle, had occupied much of his time — so much, in fact, that it has been suggested by many later scholars that it was philosophy which caused him to wander from the "straight path" and lose himself in the dark wood of his *Inferno.*

He knew well those Latin classics which were available to scholars of his time, notably Virgil, Ovid, Cicero, Seneca, Livy, and Boethius. He was familiar with much of Plato and Aristotle through Latin translations. His acquaintance with Homer was secondhand, since accounts of the Homeric heroes were circulated in Dante's time only through late Latin or medieval adaptations.

THE FIGURE OF VIRGIL

In the Middle Ages, Virgil had come to be regarded as a sage and necromancer. Virgil's poems were used in the type of divination called *sortes,* in which the book is opened at random and a verse selected in the same manner, as an answer to a problem or question. The Bible has been, and still is, used in the same manner.

Virgil's *Aeneid* offered the pattern for the structure of Dante's Hell, but this alone is not the reason why Virgil was chosen as the guide through Hell. Dante himself salutes Virgil as his master and the inspiration for his poetic style; further, Virgil is revered by Dante as the poet of the Roman Empire, since his *Aeneid* tells the story of the empire's founding. Finally, in his fourth eclogue, Virgil writes symbolically of the coming of a Wonder Child who will bring the Golden Age to the world, and in the Middle Ages this was interpreted as being prophetic of the coming of Christ. Thus, in the figure of Virgil, Dante found symbolically represented the two institutions, church and empire, destined by God to save mankind.

PLAN OF THE *COMEDY*

Dante lived in a world that believed in mystical correspondences, in which numbers — like stars, stones, and even the events of history — had a mystical significance. In planning the structure of the *Divine Comedy,* therefore, Dante had in mind a series of symbolic numbers: three, a symbol of the Holy Trinity; nine, three times three; thirty-three, a multiple of three; seven, the days of creation; ten, considered during the Middle Ages a symbol of perfection; and one hundred, the multiple of ten.

The plan was carried out with consummate precision. We find three *cantiche,* each formed by thirty-three cantos, totaling ninety-nine. The introductory first canto of the *Inferno* makes one hundred cantos in all. The entire poem is written in the difficult *terza rima,* a verse form of three-line stanzas, or tercets. The first and third lines rhyme, and the second line rhymes with the beginning line of the next stanza — again, three, and three.

Hell is divided into nine circles (in three divisions), the vestibule making the tenth; Purgatory is separated into nine levels, the terrestrial paradise making ten; and Paradise is formed by nine heavens, plus the Empyrean. The celestial hierarchies are nine and are divided into triads. The sinners in Hell are arranged according to three capital vices: incontinence, violence, and fraud. The distribution of the penitents in Purgatory is based on the threefold nature of their rational love. The partition of the blessed in Paradise is made according to the secular, active, or contemplative nature of their love for God. The very fact that each *cantica* ends with the word "stars" helps to demonstrate the studied plan of the whole work.

STRUCTURE OF INFERNO

Inferno is a huge, funnel-shaped pit located with its center beneath Jerusalem, its regions arranged in a series of circular stairsteps, or terraces, diminishing in circumference as they descend. Each of the nine regions is designated for a particular sin, and the order of the sins is according to their wickedness, the lightest near the top of the pit and the most heinous at the bottom.

The punishments in Inferno are regulated by the law of retribution; therefore, they correspond to the sins either by analogy or by antithesis. Thus, for example, the carnal sinners, who abandoned themselves to the tempests of passion, are tossed about incessantly by a fierce storm. The violent, who were bloodthirsty and vicious during their lives, are drowned in a river of blood. The sowers of dissension, who promoted social and domestic separations, are wounded and mutilated according to the nature of their crimes.

SPIRIT OF INFERNO

As soon as we enter the gate of Hell we are struck by an unforgettable vision of darkness and terror, stripped of any hope: "Abandon all hope, you who enter here," and even of the sight of the stars. In the dark,

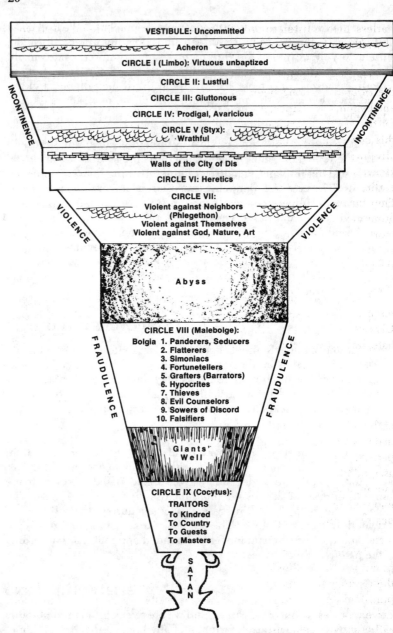

PLAN OF DANTE'S INFERNO

starless air, we listen to only "strange tongues, horrible outcries, words of wrath, and sounds of blows."

Hell is the reality of sins of the flesh, of chaos, of ugliness. And yet the *Inferno* has long been the most popular and the most widely read, and by romantic critics, it was exalted as the richest in poetry. The reason for the extraordinary fortune of the *Inferno* must be seen in the fact that this *cantica* is the closest to our world: here earthly passions are still alive in all their force, and the human character of the souls is unchanged. Heaven repudiated these souls; therefore they must remain attached to earth. Their memories, their interests and affections, their miseries, their turpitudes, their cowardice, their ugliness, seen against that background of eternity, acquire a new tragic dimension and become immortal. There is a real vitality in the *Inferno* that is lacking in the other *cantiche*, possibly because the thoughts of the age were turned less to the joys of Heaven than to the eternal damnation of Hell.

Occasionally the condemned souls are redeemed by a kind sentiment or a heroic gesture, as in the case of Paolo and Francesca, or of Ulysses. Nevertheless, Hell remains the kingdom of misery and ugliness, hate, torture, noise, and despair, without pause and without end.

STRUCTURE OF PURGATORY

Purgatory is a huge mountain located on a small island in the middle of the ocean and antipodal to Jersualem. The realm is divided into three major sections. Ante-Purgatory, at the foot of the mountain, has two parts: the mountain of Purgatory has seven ascending terraces, each assigned for one of the "seven deadly sins"; and on the summit of the mount, above Purgatory proper, is the Earthly Paradise. The sufferings endured in Purgatory are accepted voluntarily by the spirits in their desire to atone for their sins.

Penance corresponding to the sin by antithesis prevails. Thus, the proud are bowed down with heavy burdens, the lazy run without rest, the gluttons are starving. The souls are sustained by examples of the sin punished on each terrace and by its opposite virtue. The examples are carved in the stone of the mountain, chanted by invisible voices, or called aloud by the sinners themselves.

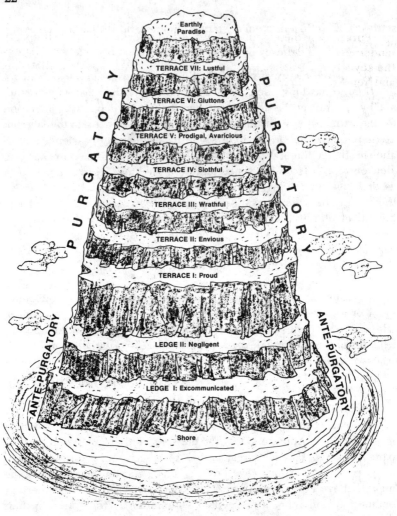

PLAN OF DANTE'S PURGATORY

SPIRIT OF PURGATORY

Upon entering the realm of Purgatory we feel a sensation of sweet and comforting relief. We return to see the sky, while a soft hue of sapphire extends to the horizon, and Venus still makes the whole East smile; we see in the distance the living surface of the sea.

Purgatory is the kingdom of peace and affection, of friendliness, of tenderness, and delicacy of feelings, of a resigned expectation. Hope is the keynote of Dante's *Purgatorio*. The souls still retain their affections and remember their earthly lives, but they do so with detachment, having in mind the new life toward which they aspire.

Earthly life and glory, seen with new eyes from the hereafter, is despoiled of all its illusions, its vanity, and its fallacious appearances. If the *Inferno* is the *cantica* richest in poetical contrast, and unforgettable because of its gallery of characters, the *Purgatorio* is certainly the richest in lyricism and nuances of color and sentiment. The souls of Purgatory are very often musical beings; they express their sensations in songs, hymns, and psalms. Purgatory is the realm of hope.

STRUCTURE OF PARADISE

Dante's representation of Paradise takes him into the heavens, heavens corresponding to the Ptolemaic system of astronomy. Circling around the earth are successive concentric spheres, each designated for a heavenly body or bodies. The first seven are the planetary spheres (including the sun and moon), and in each sphere are spirits distinguished for a particular virtue. The eighth sphere is that of the fixed stars; the ninth is outer space, called the Primum Mobile; the tenth region (not a sphere), the Empyrean, the heaven of heavens, a realm where God sits on his throne.

SPIRIT OF PARADISE

When we come to Paradise, we come to a very different world beyond earth and time. Seen from the height of Heaven, the earth has such a pitiful semblance that it makes the poet smile.

Paradise is the realm of the spirit emancipated from the senses and made completely free: the souls have forgotten earthly affections; they live only for the joy of loving and contemplating God. The sole feeling that exists in Paradise is love, the sole sensation is beatitude, the sole act is contemplation, and all these have the form of light. The *Paradiso* has very properly been called the *cantica* of light because light is the whole substance of Heaven. The souls express their thoughts by light: Beatrice shines with light every time she smiles, and the whole of Heaven changes color during the invective of St. Peter; the stages of virtues and the degrees of beatitude are also expressed by light.

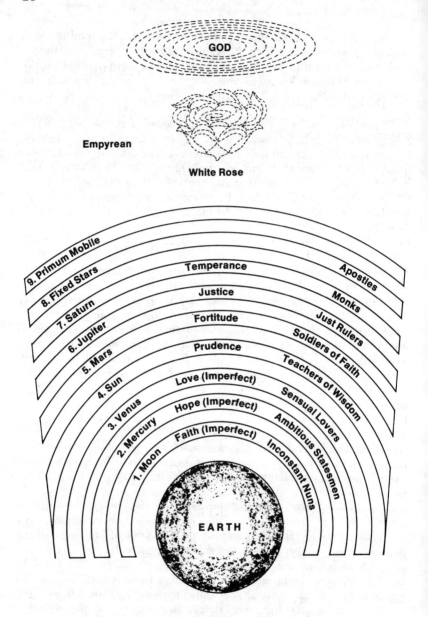

PLAN OF DANTE'S PARADISE

INTERPRETATION

The *Divine Comedy* has had many interpreters. Some have followed Dante's own thought, as outlined so clearly in his letter to Can Grande; others appear to ignore it.

Dante said plainly that the first meaning was the literal one. By this he meant that the cantos tell the story of the state of souls after death, according to the beliefs of medieval Christianity. He did *not* mean, nor intend his readers to infer, that it was a literal story of a trip through Hell, Purgatory, and Paradise; and he was safe in assuming that his audience was familiar with the literature of such journeys, a favorite subject throughout the Middle Ages. (This does not preclude reading the *Comedy* as excellent science fiction.) Hell (or Purgatory, or Paradise) is, therefore, the *condition* of the soul after death, brought to that point by the choices made during life.

Closely allied to its literal and allegorical meaning is the stated moral purpose of the *Comedy*: to point out to those yet living the error of their ways, and to turn them to the path of salvation.

Allegory is, by definition, an extended metaphor, organized in a pattern, and having a meaning separate from the literal story. C. S. Lewis has said "It is an error to suppose that in an allegory the author is 'really' talking about the thing that symbolizes; the very essence of the art is to talk about both." Aristotle believed that for a poet to have a command of metaphor was the mark of genius because it indicated a gift for seeing resemblances. This implies the gift of imagination, the ability to set down not only the images of vision, but, particularly in Dante's case, vivid images of noise and odor.

Dante wanted his reader to experience what he experienced, and from the beginning of the poem to the end he grows in power and mastery. His language is deceptively simple and so is his method. He writes in the vernacular, using all its force and directness; it is not the high poetic language of tragedy, as he said himself.

The imagery is designed to make the world of Dante's Hell intelligible to the reader. His world is the world of the thirteenth-century church, but his Hell is the creation of his mind, an allegory of redemption in which Dante seeks to show the state of the soul after death.

The poem is a demanding one. The reader must enter Dante's world without prejudice, and perhaps T. S. Eliot was right in recommending that the *Comedy* should be read straight through the first time, without giving too much attention to the background of the times, and without examining the more complex symbols.

TRANSLATION

Dante once remarked that he detested translations, thereby giving personal force to the Italian proverb *Tradutori traditori* (the translator is a traitor). To read a translation of Dante is not to read Dante, but the same may be said of Homer or Dumas or Goethe. One of the difficulties with Dante is the verse form that he used, which is not easy to render into English. The *terza rima* is a three-line stanza, as has been explained, its rhyme scheme being *aba, bcb, cdc,* etc. Often a thought will carry over from one stanza to the next. In Italian, the endings tend to be feminine (unstressed); in English they are usually masculine, or stressed. This produces basic differences in the movement and tonal quality of the poetry.

Because the *Comedy* was composed in Italian, the modern reader working with a translation is faced with certain difficulties. Each translator has put something of himself into his work. Some have written in prose, some in verse, and all have in some way interpreted as they transposed the words into English. Different teachers will recommend different versions, and of course one should follow his instructor's advice. However, the student should always remember that no single translation is definitive and that a second reading of the *Comedy,* or parts of it, in a different rendition will diminish the problems caused by the individual views of the translators.

Alice Curtayne, in her *Recall to Dante,* has devoted an entire chapter to comparative translations of the *Comedy.* She favors prose translation and gives convincing arguments for it. Dorothy Sayers, in her "Introduction" to the *Inferno,* has given some insight into the difficulties the translator faces, but unlike Miss Curtayne, believes that the *terza rima* can and should be used in English translations and demonstrates by using it in her translation of the *Comedy,* as does John Ciardi.

Paradiso Notes

INTRODUCTION TO *PARADISO*

Paradiso is the least read and, to many readers, the least successful canticle of the *Divine Comedy;* and yet it is evident that for its author it was the most important part of the poem, the capstone of the work and its greatest glory. In this respect, the final portion of the epic has suffered a fate similar to that of Goethe's *Faust, Part II,* or the second part of *Don Quixote,* and for some of the same reasons. All three are the products of the author's mature years and the receptacles of his most profound philosophy.

Although these sequels are clearly less popular and less earthy in their appeal than their antecedent works, they are esteemed superior by some serious critics; but whether one prefers the early or the later section of the work in question, all are agreed that it is impossible to deal intelligently and fairly with any of these major authors without surveying his work as a whole.

If we are to be honest in our claims for *Paradiso,* we must admit at the outset that there are difficulties for the modern reader. Certain discussions are tedious for most of us; for example, the cause of spots on the moon, the language Adam spoke, and the many Florentine families that have lost their prestige are beyond our comprehension without elaborate notes. Furthermore, the total concept of this medieval Christian heaven is quite foreign to our thought patterns.

To begin with, the student should consider the basic problem Dante faced in depicting a heaven of joy. What manner of heaven would have a universal appeal? What kinds of pleasures are suitable for a heaven that is to have a spiritual character? Earthy, sensual delights, such as the heavenly fishfry of *Green Pastures* or the refreshing Mohammedan paradise with its rich repasts and its amiable houris, are not admissible. The sensory experiences on which Dante builds his heaven are sights and sounds. The sights consist mainly of brilliant lights with their varied colors, their symbolic formations, and their gyrations. If one reverts to his own experiences in calling up imagined scenes — marching bands on a football field or the garish lights of Broadway by night —

Dante's conceptions may seem tame and amateurish. Perhaps, the best modern conceit would be a brilliant Fourth of July fireworks display. The most sensitive readers, however, come to recognize that just as Keats' unheard melodies are sweeter than those heard on earth, scenes presented to our imagination through the language of poetry may surpass the scenes of our experience.

A further problem Dante had to contend with is the fact that in our experience there are no pleasures that would not become commonplace, even boring, if prolonged indefinitely. Joy is a thing of high moments. Even the calm feeling of well-being, which has a better reputation for duration, must pass through periods of highs and lows. For this reason, the perpetual joy of Dante's saints in heaven does not call to us in compelling tones.

What we are promised in Paradise is summed up in these terms: beauty (light and music), joy, peace, and love. For Dante, the greatest of these is love, and the highest form of love is the love for God. The reward of peace, though not so positively enunciated as those other features, is woven into the entire poem. It is interesting to compare this with the final scene of Goethe's *Faust*, where the hero is elevated into heaven, and with the closing lines of the "Cantos on Mutability" at the end of Spenser's *Faerie Queene*. In both of these long and powerful works the author has demonstrated how life on earth must be a continual struggle, which is only justified, only endurable, if there is the goal of peace in victory at the end.

Ruskin declared that if *Paradiso* is less read than *Inferno* it is because "it requires far greater attention, and, perhaps for its full enjoyment, a holier heart." One may well add that it calls for greater patience but also for a deep intellectual concern and a type of imagination that goes out to meet Dante's.

PROBLEMS OF CHRONOLOGY

It is important for the reader to be alert to certain ramifications concerning the presumed date of Dante's journey through the realms of the dead, the year 1300. When he was actually engaged in writing *Paradiso*, which was between ten and twenty years after that date, people had come on the world scene and events had transpired that he felt compelled to write about. Consequently, to maintain a consistent stance, he was obliged to present everything postdating 1300 as predictions which the spirits in heaven foresee through their power to read future events.

DANTE VENTING HIS SPLEEN

A survey of *Paradiso* leaves no doubt in anyone's mind about Dante's attitude toward his contemporaries and toward the parties and institutions of his day. Those he disliked were roundly and frequently castigated through the speeches of the saints. Accordingly, Leigh Hunt maintained that the work seems more angry than celestial.

Inescapable features of the work are the poet's resentment of the papacy, with its political ambitions, and of the clergy, for their greed, stupidity, and general worldliness. Certain popes — Boniface VIII, Clement V, and John XXII — are presented as archenemies of God's kingdom on earth. So too are political leaders who struggled to obstruct the fulfillment of Dante's hope for a revival of imperial rule in Italy. Among the most hated of those figures was Philip IV, "the Fair," of France.

The explanation is simple. Dante held his convictions with passionate intensity. Moreover, he considered that it was his mission to write a poem that would benefit men of the present and future, and he believed that this could be accomplished through diverse approaches. One was to guide them through a vivid vision of penalties for sin and future glory as a reward for righteousness, but another was to sound the alarm through direct criticism of the laxity, the misdirection, and the viciousness running rife not only among leaders but even among whole nations. Obviously, the vehemence of his criticism is a calculated and important part of his message.

BEATRICE

The glorification of Beatrice — the girl Dante first saw when he was nine years old, the woman who was the object of his idealized love and the source of his inspiration during her life and after her death — is the fulfillment of the promise Dante made at the end of *La Vita Nuova:* "to write of her what has never yet been said of mortal woman." No other woman in literature has been given such a magnificent apotheosis as Beatrice here.

In her role as guide and lecturer, Beatrice stirs little enthusiasm in the reader, but neither does she provoke our antipathy because we ascribe her lectures to the Voice of Theology and accept them as expositions necessary for the unravelling of certain perplexing phenomena. The other aspect of her role in the poem is the personal treatment of a lady whom Dante loved virtually all of his life, a lady who had such love for Dante that she relinquished her seat in the Celestial Rose and descended into Hell in order to save him from his wandering in the dark wood and from the assaults of bestiality.

The passages treating Beatrice's beauty, brightness, and love constitute a tour de force of mounting intensity. Corresponding to that is the sequence expressing Dante's ever increasing feeling of love for her. The scores of passages that treat the human and personal aspect of Beatrice's role constitute a major feature of the work. Those passages, occurring in introductory or climactic situations are the most appealing, the most memorable, and the most poetic passages in the epic.

The major theme of the *Comedy* is the rich reward that is attained by a mortal through his love of God. But how can the poet make us understand that kind of love? The ladder on which we must mount to that understanding is the love of a fellow human being. Thus we recognize how vital the role of Beatrice is to this great poem.

SYNOPSIS

The poet announces the theme of this climactic canticle as the ineffable vision of heaven, whereupon he invokes the aid of the muses and Apollo for inspiration and eloquence.

The time is high noon on the Mountain of Purgatory and the season is the vernal equinox, the most propitious time of the year. Dante, having been instructed and purified in Purgatory, is prepared for his journey to Paradise. Seeing Beatrice lift her glance toward the sun, he follows her example and is at that moment transformed ("transhumanized") in preparation for his great adventure. He is surprised to discover a new brightness and wonderful music around them, until Beatrice explains that they have flown, swifter than thought, up to the *Sphere of Fire,* and that his new state (transhumanized) permits him to hear the music of the spheres.

After a flight of incredible speed, the travelers arrive in the first heaven, the *Sphere of the Moon*. Because the sphere is composed of matter, Dante has difficulty understanding how he can penetrate that body, and he speculates on whether or not he is in his corporeal state.

The age-old question of the cause of the spots on the moon is treated at length. Beatrice asks Dante for his conjecture regarding the puzzle, but she refutes his theory and then proceeds to expound the real cause of the appearance of those apparent blemishes.

Through the pearly, diaphanous substance of the sphere, the poet perceives the faces of spirits. One of these identifies herself as Piccarda Donati, a former acquaintance. She tells him that she is in this region because she was forced to violate her vow of chastity and to marry a man she hated. Consequently, she has been consigned to this, the lowest stage of blessedness; but she assures him that all the souls in Paradise are perfectly contented with whatever degree of blessedness God has willed for them. A companion of Piccarda is then introduced, the Empress Constance, mother of Frederick II. Like Piccarda, she was withdrawn from her convent and forced into marriage.

In answer to a problem worrying Dante, Beatrice explains that all the heavenly spirits have their permanent abode in the Empyrean, the highest heaven; but for Dante's instruction different categories of spirits will descend and appear for him in one of the planetary spheres with which they are associated through their distinguishing virtue.

Several problems concerning vows, about which Dante has some doubts, are explained at length for him by his instructress, questions concerning the responsibility for vows broken under duress, and the possibility of substituting new acts of righteousness for the one originally pledged.

Suddenly Dante becomes aware that they have arrived in a new region, the *Sphere of Mercury*. Beatrice's countenance has acquired a new radiance, which is a sign of her increased delight, the result of the ascension. The souls in this region appear as glowing lights; neither their faces nor other physical features are recognizable. (This is a condition of all the remaining spirits in the heavenly spheres except those in the Empyrean.)

In response to Dante's query, a spirit identifies himself as Justinian, the emperor who was the author and sponsor of the Roman legal code.

He proudly surveys the history of the Roman Empire, citing great figures and major events with an emphasis on the important role of imperial rule as part of the divine plan for mankind.

He further explains that the company of spirits assembled in Mercury are those who were so absorbed in their pursuit of fame and honor that they neglected their religious duties. He then identifies one of his companion spirits as Romeo da Villanova, a devoted minister of a count of Provence, who unjustly suffered disgrace and exile.

Justinian's discourse leaves Dante with certain questions about the Crucifixion which Beatrice undertakes to explain for him. She distinguishes two aspects of the Crucifixion based on the dual nature of Christ. She further expounds upon the nature of redemption and affirms the final resurrection of the body.

Seeing Beatrice become yet more lovely, Dante realizes that they have soared into a new heaven, the *Sphere of Venus*. One spirit, advancing from the dancing lights, addresses Dante as a former acquaintance. He is Charles Martel of the Anjou dynasty. A discussion of heredity follows, which, in turn, leads to a treatment of the problem of celestial influences that endow individuals with diverse dispositions and capabilities.

Other persons who are identified among the spirits in Venus (Cunizza, Folco, and Rahab the Harlot) are all persons who in early life "burned with amorous fire" but later were converted to true *caritas,* or divine love. Their discourse, however, is chiefly aimed at the degeneracy of contemporary political and religious life—Cunizza's against her native Treviso, Folco's against Florence and the papacy.

The arrival of the pilgrims in the *Sphere of the Sun,* the heaven of wisdom, is marked by a surrounding light of indescribable brilliance. At first they are circled by a ring of twelve dancing lights singing in harmonious tones. One spirit offers to name the members of the circle. He is St. Thomas Aquinas, and his companions include some of the great sages, teachers, and theologians—among them, Albertus Magnus, Solomon, Boethius, the Venerable Bede, Orosius, and Dionysius the Areopagite.

As the circle of saints pauses, Aquinas relates the story of St. Francis of Assisi: how he foreswore his wealthy heritage and took a strict vow of poverty, how he founded the order of Franciscan friars, how he preached to the Sultan, and how he received the stigmata. Aquinas then speaks disparagingly of his own order, the Dominicans, many of whom, he bitterly reports, have forsaken the high purpose of their leader.

As Aquinas ends his speech, a second circle of twelve lights appears outside the first. Their spokesman, Bonaventura, who was a prominent Franciscan leader, relates the story of the life of St. Dominic: his Spanish birth, his eloquent preaching, his battles against heresy, and his powerful influence on Christianity through the foundation of his order. Bonaventura then denounces his own brother Franciscans for their laxity and degeneracy.

The second circle of sages includes, in addition to Bonaventura, Nathan the Prophet, Hugh of St. Victor, Chrysostom, Anselm, and Donatus, as well as the earliest disciples of St. Francis.

Aquinas, discussing a point about the superior wisdom of Solomon, explains that Christ and Adam are exempt from comparison with other men because they were created by God, whereas all other humans are created by God's ministers, the Intelligences in the stars. Solomon then resolves one further problem puzzling Dante concerning the reuniting of bodies and souls at the Resurrection. Suddenly, a third circle of light appears surrounding the other two. No spirits of this circle are named, but the emblem of the three rings stands for the Trinity and foreshadows the climactic vision in the Empyrean.

Arriving in a new realm, the *Sphere of Mars*, the voyagers perceive two streams of light that intersect to form a great cross, within which they momentarily see a vision of Christ. The lights composing the cross sing a martial hymn which at first Dante does not fully understand.

One spirit descends to the foot of the cross to speak to the poet. It is Cacciaguida, his great-great-grandfather, who fought and died as a crusader under the Emperor Conrad. He praises Florence as she was in his day, a city which was distinguished for its plain and sober living and reverence for moral customs. When pressed for more details by the poet, Cacciaguida gives the time of his birth (about 1100) but refuses to discuss his ancestry. He notes that the population of Florence, which has increased five times, has deteriorated in the character of its citizens because of the incursion of inferior stock from surrounding towns and farms; and he cites numerous families once prominent in Florence but now of little note.

To satisfy Dante's question regarding the misfortunes that he has been told are in store for him, Cacciaguida, in a moving speech, describes the conditions of Dante's life in exile, but he also promises some relief through the generous patronage of the della Scala family, and he further predicts punishment for those responsible for Dante's exile.

Finally, the old crusader identifies a few of the distinguished warriors who are among his companions in this sphere: Joshua, Judas Maccabeus, Charlemagne, Roland, and Godfrey of Bouillon.

A glance toward Beatrice, whose features show an added brightness, tells Dante that they have risen to a new region, the *Sphere of Jupiter*. A series of swimming lights spells out, letter by letter, a biblical message on justice: DILIGITE IUSTICIAM . . . TERRAM ("Love justice, ye that judge the earth"). The final letter of the message, M, lingers but is then transformed, first to the emblem of a lily and then to an eagle, the symbol of the Empire. Contemplating the relationship between heavenly and earthly justice, Dante inveighs against the reigning pope for his abuse of earthly justice.

The band of spirits forming the eagle addresses Dante in unison. When he asks for an explanation of divine justice, he is told that its nature is beyond human comprehension. One issue which especially worries Dante concerns the fate of virtuous heathens. He is told that these souls may attain a better place in glory than factitious worshipers of Christianity.

The eagle denounces numerous sovereigns who have perverted justice: Emperor Albert of Austria, Philip the Fair of France, Edward I of England, and most of the other living rulers.

An interval of glorious song follows. Then the eagle designates some of the noblest souls in its formation—those marking its eye and brow. In the pupil of the eye is King David; the five souls forming the eyebrow are: the Emperor Trajan, Hezekiah, the Emperor Constantine, William II of Sicily, and Ripheus the Trojan. It has to be explained to Dante how two of those persons were included, since he supposed that they were not Christians. Trajan, he is informed, was miraculously restored to life through Pope Gregory I's intercession and converted to the faith. Ripheus was granted foreknowledge of Christ and believed.

Upon arrival in the *Sphere of Saturn*, Dante sees a golden ladder upon which angel lights are mounting and descending. These are spirits who devoted their lives to contemplation.

A spirit descends to greet Dante, identifying himself as Peter Damian, a monk renowned for asceticism. He dismisses predestination as
beyond man's comprehension and he castigates the present-day clergy
for having grown fat and rich. All of the spirits present join him in a
thunderous shout of approval.

A second light approaches and addresses the poet. It is St. Benedict,
who founded the order of Benedictine monks and the famous monastery
at Monte Cassino. He decries the decay of the true monastic spirit
among his living followers, whom he labels "a den of thieves." They
ignore the path of contemplation, which, like the golden ladder, leads
upward toward God.

As Benedict and the host of lights mount the golden ladder, Dante
is directed by Beatrice to follow. Thus the pilgrims attain the *Sphere of
Fixed Stars*. From their new height Dante looks back down to earth;
and, noting how tiny and inconsequential it appears from that distance,
he is led to reflect upon the vanity of all worldly goals.

Following Beatrice's example of gazing heavenward, Dante is
greeted with a vision of Christ. The brilliance of Christ's image is too
great for him to bear, and he is forced to lower his eyes. Beatrice bids
him to look at her, then she smiles and he looks up again. Christ has
soared to heaven and now Mary appears surrounded by a host of the
blessed—the prophets and the apostles. Gabriel leads the host in paying
solemn tribute to her.

When Mary has followed her Son toward the Empyrean, St. Peter
detaches himself from the throng of lights and proceeds to examine
Dante on his understanding of faith. Finding the responses wholly
satisfactory, the saint expresses his delight. A second light, St. James,
descends to examine the candidate on hope, and Dante discourses on
hope to the eminent satisfaction of St. James and the attendant host. A
third spirit approaches, St. John, who examines Dante on love. Dante
explains that his understanding of love is based on both reason and
revelation. The greatest bond of his love of God is Christ's sacrifice. The
assembly of spirits greets his responses with "Holy, holy, holy!"

Finally Adam appears before Dante and answers questions that
have long puzzled biblical students: how long did Adam dwell in the
Garden before his banishment? how long did he live on earth? how
long was he in Limbo? and, finally, what language did he speak?

Before the departure of the apostles, St. Peter delivers a vehement denunciation of his recent successors in the papal seat (Clement V and John XXII), who have turned his tomb into "a sewer of blood and filth."

As Dante and Beatrice enter the ninth sphere, the *Primum Mobile,* Beatrice explains that it is this sphere that drives the motion of all the lower spheres. Here the poet will witness a vision of God and His relation to the angels. Dante sees a dot of intense brilliance surrounded by a series of concentric rings of light. Beatrice explains that the circles represent the classes of angels and that they receive their light and force in proportion to their nearness to God, the central light. The classes of angels are named in the order of their virtue, from greatest to least: Seraphim, Cherubim, Thrones, Dominations, Virtues, Powers, Principalities, Archangels, and Angels. The angels are also designated as Intelligences, and each order sheds its influence on one of the spheres below.

Beatrice answers two questions concerning angels: whether they existed before the Creation, and whether they possess memory as well as understanding and will.

Dante again turns to Beatrice, and he tells us that if all he has ever said of her beauty could be compounded it could not express the beauty she has now attained. She announces their arrival in the *Empyrean,* the region of pure light; and she informs Dante that he will be privileged to see the saints in their corporeal forms as they will appear on the day of the Resurrection.

At first he sees a river of light between flowery banks, but as he dips his eyes in that river, it is transformed into a great rose at whose center is a wonderful source of light. The petals are formed with row on row of saints in glory. Beatrice points out to him that there are few unfilled places. She then calls his attention to the throne reserved for the Emperor Henry VII.

The blessed souls clad in white raiment fill the great rose. Angels fly, like a swarm of bees, up from the heart of the rose to the petals, their faces of living flame, their wings of gold, their bodies white as purest snow.

After gazing at the mystic scene, Dante turns to speak to Beatrice but discovers that she is no longer beside him. In her place is a saintly elder, St. Bernard, who points out Beatrice where now she has resumed her honored place in the rose. Bernard then enjoins Dante to look up to the highest tier where Mary sits enthroned, surrounded by a thousand joyful angels.

The arrangement of the principal souls in the Celestial Rose is explained by Bernard. Directly below the Virgin are heroines of the Old Testament: Eve, Rachel (beside her is Beatrice), Sarah, Rebecca, Judith, and Ruth. On the opposite side of the rose in a similar vertical arrangement are the male figures of the Christian era: John the Baptist, St. Francis, St. Benedict, and St. Augustine. Seated to one side or the other of Mary are: Adam, Peter, Moses and John the Apostle; flanking John the Baptist are St. Anne and St. Lucy. All of the upper rows of petals are occupied by adult figures, whereas the lower tiers are filled with infants.

St. Bernard now delivers a memorable apostrophe and prayer to the Virgin, praising her for her benign spirit, then pleading for her intercession on Dante's behalf that he may be permitted the Beatific Vision. With a gracious smile she signals her consent, and Dante lifts his eyes toward the light at the heart of the rose. What he saw he can report only in faintly recollected form, so potent was the experience. Within one blinding light he recognized three separate lights in the form of interlocking circles (a symbol of the Trinity), and within one circle he perceived the dim image of a human face, a reminder that God, through Christ, lived—and still lives—as man on earth.

At this point the poet comprehended the oneness of the manifold pages in the book of the universe; he felt desire and will brought into conformity.

SUMMARIES AND COMMENTARIES

CANTO 1

Summary

God's glory, which is resplendent through all the universe, shines more brightly in one part and less brightly in another. In the part of heaven that receives His brightest light, Dante has stood, but it is impossible for one who has returned from there to tell the wonder of it fully. Still, what his memory retains of that treasured experience will be the theme of his song.

He solemnly invokes Apollo to give him power to speak of that blessed realm in fitting terms. Now he needs the support of both peaks of Parnassus; now he needs the eloquence which gave Apollo victory in his contest with Marsyas. He pledges to strive for the crown of laurel, which is too seldom sought in his time.

The sun, which has risen in its most beneficent position—that is, in the sign of Aries and about the time of the vernal (spring) equinox— is lighting all the hemisphere of Purgatory, where Dante stands with Beatrice. When he sees Beatrice look directly at the sun, Dante follows her example and is able to endure the brightness better than mortal eyes can normally do. Sparks like hot iron boil out of the sun's fire. Then suddenly the day seems doubly bright. Dante turns and fixes his gaze on Beatrice, and as he looks at her he becomes transhumanized— like Glaucus, who was transformed into a sea god after eating a certain herb. He cannot say if in that state he existed physically or was only "that part of me created first," the rational human soul.

The sounds of harmony and the intense brightness that surround them bewilder the poet, whereupon Beatrice offers an explanation. His confusion is caused by his failure to realize that they have left the earth and have risen to the Sphere of Fire; his soul has sped swifter than lightning toward "its home." It is the law of the universe, she declares, that all things, animate and inanimate, move by instinct toward their natural abode. As fire rises toward heaven, so the pure soul rises to God. For Dante, now that he has been purified, it should not be a surprise that he is soaring heavenward.

Commentary

In opening the account of his journey through Paradise, Dante leaves no doubt that the adventure he is about to relate transcends all other experiences. God's glory shines more radiantly in the Empyrean, the heaven of heavens, than in any other part of the universe, and Dante says, "I was there." To reveal that glory fully is beyond human power, but he will tell as much of that experience as his memory holds. To aid him in this endeavor, he invokes Apollo and the muses for the gift of eloquence. Whereas in *Inferno* and *Purgatorio* he called upon the muses only, he now adds his appeal to Apollo. The twin peaks of Mount Parnassus to which he refers were sacred to those divinities, one to Apollo and the other to the muses. He made the distinction earlier (*La Vita Nuova*) between the muses as directors of the poet's science, or art, and Apollo as the giver of divine inspiration. In his invocation to Apollo,

Dante recalls the contest in which Apollo defeated the satyr Marsyas in a musical contest; and he also refers to the legend of Daphne, who was turned into a laurel tree; because the tree was henceforth sacred to Apollo, wreaths of laurel were used to crown both poets and victorious generals.

If the reader is surprised or shocked to discover that in a poem of such intense Christian dedication the author should call upon a pagan god for inspiration, he must remember that for Dante the model for noble poetry was the classical epic and thus the formalities of epic poetry were prized props for him, as indeed they were for many later Christian poets.

The time for the beginning of the flight toward heaven, the poet notes, is most propitious. The sun is lighting all of the hemisphere of Purgatory, which is to say that it is noon there. Furthermore, it is the best time of the year, the vernal equinox (the time of year when God, it was believed, created the world) and the time when the sun exerts its greatest influence on earth—"stamps the wax of the world with its temper." The reference to the four circles joined to three crosses specifies that the line of the equator, the ecliptic (of the zodiac), and the horizon intersect at the equinoctial colure (the great circle traversing the two poles). Their intersecting forms the crosses.

When Dante sees Beatrice turn her face up toward the sun, he does the same and discovers that his eyes can now sustain its brightness. He soon perceives that they are surrounded by a double brightness (the Sphere of Fire that is between the Sphere of the Earth and the Sphere of the Moon) and that harmonious sounds fill the air (the music of the spheres); still, however, he does not understand that they have risen high into the heavens. Beatrice explains how it is that he has soared swifter than lightning. Since his soul was purified in Purgatory and all sin was cast off, it is free to obey a basic law of the universe which dictates that the pure soul is drawn by instinct toward God.

CANTO 2

Summary

The poet addresses his readers and, using a striking nautical metaphor, warns all who have been following his ship to turn back, for his journey will now take him far out over the unknown, dangerous deep; but he invites those who have been striving for "the bread of angels" to follow, keeping close in his wake, and he promises that they will see much to amaze them.

Dante and Beatrice, borne upward as swiftly as a glance by their thirst for heaven, arrive in a new region of heaven with the speed of an arrow from a crossbow. They have entered the Sphere of the Moon. Dante wonders how his body can enter into that pearly, solid substance that surrounds them — if indeed he is a body now — for that appears to contradict the laws of science. After serious consideration, he discovers that the phenomenon helps to illuminate the mystery of Christ's incarnation.

When he asks Beatrice the cause of the dark spots on the moon, she asks what his opinion is. He advances the theory that different portions of the planet are of different density. Beatrice, in refuting that theory, reasons that the light from the Sphere of Fixed Stars is affected by something far different than the magnitude or density of various stars. Different stars possess different virtues, hence their differences in intensity and color. Against Dante's variable density theory, she further suggests that if the areas of rarified matter extended clear through the moon, the sun's light ought to show through at the time of an eclipse. She also refutes another theory which had been proposed to the effect that the rarified regions were of variable depths and that light rays were reflected from the bottom of those depressions and consequently were dimmer than those reflected from the planet's surface because they came from a greater distance. To show the fallacy of that concept, Beatrice proposes a simple experiment: place two mirrors equidistant from an observer and place a third mirror farther away, then have a light held behind him so that he can observe the reflection in the mirrors. He will discover that the image in the farther mirror is as bright as the other images.

The explanation of the true cause of the spots involves an account of the manner in which energy and light are transmitted throughout the universe, deriving from God and carried from the Primum Mobile down through the lower spheres. The energy and light transmitted are uniform, but the results of their impact on various heavenly bodies differ in accordance with the nature or essence of the body. The differences, then, are not differences of quantity but of quality; by the same reasoning, the differences found in the light on the moon are caused by variations in the essences of different regions.

Commentary

The ship mentioned at the opening of this canto is a counterpart to one at the beginning of *Purgatorio* (Canto 1). Since the basis of Dante's narrative is a journey, it is to be expected that he will draw many similes and metaphors from different modes of travel: pilgrimages, riding, climbing, swimming, sailing, and even flying. In this passage, he tries to discourage the majority of readers — those in small boats — from reading further. Only those who have cultivated a love for "the bread of angels" — a biblical phrase meaning spiritual understanding (Psalms 78) — are encouraged to venture out on this ocean. The reference to the men who crossed the sea to Colchis, the Argonauts, and their surprise at Jason's turning plowman is apt in its context, and it is also interesting for its associative juxtaposition to the nautical metaphor just mentioned.

The substance of the sphere of the first planet, the moon, is solid and pearl-like. The puzzle as to how two bodies can occupy the same space causes Dante to speculate. "If I was then a body," he says, "how could that body enter the solid body of the moon's sphere?" He manages to turn this speculation into a revelation of the mystery of Christ's being God and man in one.

A lengthy discussion now follows about the spots on the moon. This was a subject of serious concern to astronomers and philosophers before Galileo's dramatic view through his telescope, three centuries after Dante, revealed mountains and valleys, craters and fissures on its surface. The theory of varying densities was one that had been espoused by such scholars as Averroes and Albertus Magnus and which Dante had sanctioned in his Convivio. The refutation of that theory and the presentation of a new theory, although propounded by Beatrice, represents Dante's more mature judgment on the question.

To understand the argument about the different essences in the various stars, planets, and constellations, we must recall that scientists believed then in the diverse influences exerted on men's lives by the individual heavenly bodies. The discussion of the problem of the moon's spots, which must seem to modern readers not only tedious but even silly, serves Dante as the occasion for introducing a much more important concept — that is, the design of the force that drives and animates the universe.

The long and, to us, theoretical discourse of this canto is the beginning of that hard and dangerous intellectual voyage about which we were warned, the voyage that will explore the mysteries of God's universal plan.

CANTO 3

Summary

In the pearly atmosphere of the moon, Dante notices seven faces that seem eager to speak to him. The faces appear so diaphanous that at first he supposes that he is looking at hazy reflections, but Beatrice assures him that they are true substances, spirits whose status is represented by this sphere. She encourages Dante to speak to them.

When Dante addresses one of the spirits asking who she is, she replies that she is Piccarda, whom he should recognize even though she is more beautiful than she was on earth. She explains that all of the spirits in this region are in this lowest sphere because they broke their vows to God or failed in complete fulfillment of them, but she assures Dante of their contentment. He asks if they aspire to rise eventually to a higher station, at which Piccarda and her companions smile, declaring that their happiness is complete because they occupy the status chosen for them by divine love. "In His will is our peace." Through this revelation, Dante comes to understand that though God's grace is bestowed on different souls in different degrees, all of the blessed spirits are perfectly happy in their various degree of blessedness.

Piccarda relates that after she had taken religious vows and entered the order of St. Clare, she was taken from her convent against her will and forced by one of her brothers to marry Rossellino della Tosa.

Beside Piccarda is another spirit, whom she identifies as "the great Constance." The experience of Constance was much the same as Piccarda's; she was forced to leave her holy order and to enter into marriage. Her husband is referred to as one of those representing "the wind out of Swabia" (the Swabian dynasty of the Empire). Although the veil was snatched from Constance's brow, Piccarda declares, she always wore it in her heart.

As Piccarda sings an *Ave Maria*, her image fades as though she were sinking ever deeper into water. Losing sight of her, Dante turns to Beatrice, but now her face appears so glowing that he cannot at first endure its brightness.

Commentary

In Dante's journey through the heavens he will meet groups of spirits in each successive sphere; thus the narrative of the journey through Paradise parallels the narrative structures of *Inferno* and *Purgatorio,* in which he passed from circle to circle and terrace to terrace meeting special groups of spirits. The classification of the groups in Paradise is governed by the virtue associated with the sphere involved, the virtues being arranged in an ascending order of holiness. The spirits in the first three spheres are the least sanctified because their virtues include some taint of earthliness, just as those planets nearest the earth — the Moon, Mercury, and Venus — sometimes come under the shadow of the earth in an eclipse.

The spirits who appear to Dante here seem like indistinct reflections or images seen dimly underwater. In the higher regions of heaven, the bodily forms of the spirits are entirely indistinguishable and they are seen only as bright lights.

The virtue associated with the moon is faith. The spirits consigned to this sphere were distinguished by that virtue on earth, but failed to achieve perfection. They were guilty of broken vows. The fact that they were victims of violent enforcement and did not willingly betray their faith must, however, be considered as a mitigating circumstance in judging their merits. Their degree of blessedness is the least of all the heavenly spirits, but to them it constitutes perfect contentment and they aspire to no higher condition. Their will is identical with the will of God, and their happiness is summed up in the famous speech, "In His will is our peace" *(E'n la sua volontade è nostra pace).*

The first spirit to converse with Dante is Piccarda Donati, whom Dante knew in her lifetime. She was a relative of his wife and the sister of his friend Forese (cf. *Purg.* 23, 24). It was Piccarda's other brother, the notorious Corso Donati, who acted the villain in this adventure, invading Piccarda's convent and forcing her into a marriage of convenience. Dante's deep-seated animosity toward Corso may have no particular bearing on this episode, but it will be recalled that Corso was a leader of the "Black" party in the revolt that brought about Dante's exile.

A second spirit, appearing beside Piccarda, is introduced to Dante as "the great Constance," an empress of the Holy Roman Empire (mentioned in *Purg.* 3). In identifying Constance, Piccarda speaks of the second and third winds that came out of Swabia, a reference to the Swabian dynasty — Frederick I (Barbarossa), Henry VI, and Frederick II. She calls them "winds" because of their reputations for extraordinary energy. The story of the life of Constance is similar to Piccarda's since she was said to have been abducted from her convent to be married to the prince who later became Emperor Henry VI — "the second wind" — and she was the mother of Frederick II.

It is no accident that an empress stands beside a woman of citizen status without regard for the regal or aristocratic rank of earthly life. In heaven, such earthly distinctions no longer have validity. This same kind of abrogation of social rank is demonstrated in almost every one of the regions of Paradise.

The canto closes, as it opened, with a reference to the radiance of Beatrice in Dante's sight.

CANTO 4

Summary

At the end of his meeting with Piccarda and Constance, Dante is perplexed by two questions, but unable to decide which to broach first, he stands mute. Beatrice, knowing his thoughts, offers to resolve his problems. The first concern she treats is whether all of the souls in heaven inhabit a sphere from which they came to earth and from which they derived their character, as Plato maintained, or whether all have their heavenly abodes in the Empyrean. Beatrice declares that those spirits they have just seen and, indeed, *all* of the blessed dwell in the Empyrean together with the Seraphim and the saints, and with Moses, Samuel, the two Johns, and Mary. They are shown to Dante in the sphere with which they are associated spiritually in order to make clear to Dante the different kinds and degrees of blessedness among the heavenly spirits. This method for instructing Dante is adopted, Beatrice explains, because in dealing with the human intellect, perception through the senses is necessary for understanding. She says that Plato expressed the belief that souls return to the stars from which they came before their earthly existence, but he was in error in this matter, unless his words were intended to convey a hidden meaning; that is, Plato's theories were always taken literally. Beatrice comments that Plato *may* have been speaking symbolically. Since, however, no one considered this possibility, the result was that most nations named the planets for false gods — Jupiter, Mercury, and Mars.

The second problem worrying Dante concerns whether or not it is just to blame someone for an action that is forced upon him against his will. Beatrice points out that the "perfect will" does not die in a person; if one accepts a condition under duress, he will return to his true position at the first opportunity. The fault lies *not* in the original act but in the ultimate *acceptance* of the new role, as in the case of those ladies who, when forced to break their religious vows, failed to return to the convent when they were free to do so. This seems to bring into question Piccarda's remark that Constance kept her love for the veil always in her heart. Beatrice points out that one must recognize the distinction between the will that is checked by fear or some other counterforce and the type of will which surmounts all fear or pain, as that of St. Lawrence, for example.

Dante expresses his keen gratitude to Beatrice for her instruction and then asks one more question: can one pay the debt for the breaking of vows by performing virtuous deeds? Thereupon, Beatrice looks at Dante with eyes so bright that he is forced to turn his glance away.

Commentary

The present canto is wholly didactic, being concerned with matters of interpretation regarding what was seen and heard in the previous canto. Dante's indecision as to which question he should ask first, described by a series of figures of speech, represents what medieval logicians called the dilemma of Buridan's ass, the ass that stands between two bales of hay, debating which to eat first.

Beatrice, reading Dante's mind, proceeds to answer the questions, taking up the more dangerous problem first: do certain souls in heaven inhabit certain spheres or do all dwell in the Empyrean before the throne of God? Plato, in his dialogue *Timaeus*, maintained that before birth every soul inhabits a star that casts its influence over the individual temperament and the soul returns to that star after death if its earthly life was well ordered. Since the doctrine had so notable an author, and since it was supported by Cicero, Dante evidently felt that it had to be taken into account. Beatrice says that *all* souls dwell in the Empyrean and that Plato's doctrine is in error if interpreted literally; but she suggests that Plato may have intended his statement in an allegorical sense. In any case, she points out, many people have been misguided by it; and, attaching stellar influence to souls at birth, they named the planets for pagan gods and goddesses.

The reason given for having certain spirits show themselves to Dante in a particular sphere is that this presentation will make more readily understandable the hierarchy of the souls in Paradise. Human intellect requires sensory demonstration. By this arrangement, the poet has, in fact, applied Plato's concept of souls residing in their proper spheres although he rejected it for theological purposes.

Dante's second perplexity, which Beatrice now offers to resolve, concerns the problem of justice for those who are forced to abandon a way of life to which they were dedicated and are nevertheless held guilty. Their guilt, she explains, lies in their resigning themselves to the new way of life and failing to return to their former life when they are free to do so. Concerning Piccarda and Constance, she says that their absolute will dictated that they should return to the veil; but their "conditioned will" permitted them to make concessions to external pressures which threatened distasteful or disastrous consequences. These ladies chose the easier way, the compromise, in contrast to St. Lawrence, who, through adherence to his absolute will, accepted martyrdom.

Piccarda spoke the truth, Beatrice says, when she declared that the love of the veil was always in Constance's heart. This love in her heart was a response to her absolute will, but her conditioned will allowed her to accept her new role throughout the rest of her life.

After expressing his intense gratitude to Beatrice for her elucidations, Dante proposes one further question, the answer to which is delayed until the following canto.

CANTO 5

Summary

Beatrice first explains the increase in her brightness, which has momentarily blinded Dante. As joy increases, it is expressed in greater light; therefore, as she perceives his growth in spiritual insight, she is pleased and so gives forth a greater brilliance. She then proceeds to answer his latest question about the possibility of compensating for broken vows by performing good works. She reminds him that man's most precious possession is his free will, and she explains that a vow to God constitutes one's sacrifice of that free will, and that nothing can equal that most precious possession. Therefore, good deeds can never compensate fully for breaking one's vow. But to go into the matter more deeply, she explains that there are two parts to the vow, the act of promising and the things promised. The promise itself cannot be withdrawn, but the things promised, the deeds one pledges, can be replaced by other deeds; but when such a substitution is performed, it requires formal sanction through Church authority (the turning of the white key and the yellow). Furthermore, the deeds offered in compensation must be in a ratio to the original pledge of six to four.

A further distinction, according to Beatrice, must be drawn between the vow which is acceptable to God and one that is unacceptable, for the vow must be regarded as a compact between two parties. If a vow is unreasonable, God would reject it; hence, it should not be fulfilled. Jephthah the Israelite should have realized the fallacy of his pledge and retracted it rather than executing it. The same reasoning can be applied in the case of Agamemnon, who sacrificed his daughter Iphigenia because of his ill-considered vow.

Beatrice then exhorts all Christians to be cautious in the making of vows and urges obedience to both the Old and the New Testaments. Follow your Good Shepherd, she says, and avoid the tempter who may lead you astray like foolish sheep.

Suddenly the poet and his guide are transported to the second planetary sphere. The joy of Beatrice creates such radiance that she causes the sphere to glow more brightly, and Dante's delight is likewise responsive to her radiance. He sees crowding toward them more than a thousand bright souls, "a thousand splendors," and hears them say, "Behold one who will increase our loves." One of the leading spirits addresses Dante as someone granted exceptional grace to visit heaven while still alive and invites him to question them. Dante replies that he understands how they are concealed in their own brightness and that he detects their smiles by the added sparks from their eyes, but he cannot recognize them. He begs them to tell who they are and how they come to be associated with this sphere. The spirit to whom Dante spoke begins to glow more brightly than before as he prepares to address the poet.

Commentary

The explanation of Beatrice's brightness involves a spiritual law. Joy, which depends on love, increases with one's understanding or spiritual vision, and that increase in joy is expressed in added brightness. Beatrice has grown brighter because of her apprehension of Dante's growing insight into divine truth.

The discourse that follows concerning religious vows has been judged by some critics to be more thorough than the subject deserves.

The reason for Dante's giving it so much attention may be, as Grandgent has suggested, that the subject was of particular interest to the poet because, according to an old tradition, he at one time seriously considered entering the Franciscan order.

It is to be noted that Dante has seasoned the abstract discourse with concrete examples and literary allusions. To illustrate the distinction between the act of promising and the things promised, Beatrice introduces the comparison with the Hebrew sacrifices. The Hebrews were bound to perform the sacrifice, but the thing sacrificed could be changed. So with respect to Christian vows, the vow may not be retracted but the deeds promised may be substituted, though only under ecclesiastical dispensation. The reference to the authority of dispensations delegated to the Church is couched in the phrase "the turning of the white key and the yellow" (the silver and gold keys). The allusion is to the keys held by the angel guarding the gate to Purgatory (*Purg.* 9).

As examples of vows that ought not to have been binding because they were not accepted by God, Beatrice produces one biblical and one classical instance. Jephthah vowed that if God granted his army victory he would sacrifice the first living creature that came out to greet him upon his return home. When his daughter met him, he was painfully grieved but he considered his vow to be binding. Under somewhat similar circumstances, Agamemnon sacrificed his daughter Iphigenia to Artemis to obtain favoring winds to blow the Greek fleet to Troy.

In Beatrice's warning to mankind, "If you are tempted by greed to stray from the guidance of your Shepherd, . . ." the suggested interpretation is, "If you are tempted by fake pardoners to take your vows lightly because you can buy pardons for a fee, don't be led astray like silly sheep."

Dante again notes the phenomenon of the increasing of Beatrice's brightness and his own as they advance to the new region. The second sphere, that of Mercury, is not directly named in this passage, an instance of the type of intellectual game that Dante plays with his readers. Those who can will be pleased to supply the name themselves.

The spirits here appear simply as spots of light, no features or bodily forms being recognizable, and such is the case throughout the remaining regions of Paradise, with the exception of the Empyrean.

The first words spoken by the spirits, "Behold one who will increase our love," is an echo of the doctrine concerning spiritual possessions, which was expounded in *Purgatorio* 15, to the effect that the more souls there are loving God, the more His love is poured out to all.

The spirit, not yet identified, who first spoke to Dante, increases in splendor at the poet's address to him. And thus the canto ends on the theme with which it opened, the instance of a spirit gaining in brightness with increase of love — love that is derived from increased spiritual sight.

CANTO 6

Summary

The spirit addressing Dante identifies himself as Justinian, the sixth-century emperor. Justinian's greatest achievement, the codification of Roman law, was accomplished, he explains, only after he was freed from heresy by the pope and instructed in the dual nature (human and divine) of Christ. To enlighten Dante further, he reviews the high points in the history of the empire, basing his history on the movements of the Roman eagle as the symbol of the empire. He cites the westward voyage of Aeneas to establish the new Troy in Italy, the adventures of the Horatii, the defeat of Hannibal, the wars of Caesar and Pompey, Augustus as first emperor, Tiberius as third emperor in whose reign Christ was crucified, the vengeance under Titus against the Jews for the Crucifixion, and the defense of Rome by Charlemagne against the barbarian Lombards. Concluding his report of the past glories of the Roman eagle, Justinian points out the evil course of present factions within the empire tending toward the weakening or even tearing down of the eagle. The Guelfs under "the new Charles" are hoping to substitute the lilies of France for the eagle, and the Ghibellines wish to claim the eagle as the emblem of their faction exclusively.

To answer Dante's second question regarding the character of the spirits consigned to the sphere of Mercury, Justinian explains that these were virtuous persons who became so absorbed in gaining fame and honor that they neglected their devotion and service to God. He expresses their contentment with their degree of blessedness, which they recognize as fitting for their natures.

One of the spirits is identified by Justinian as Romèo, a man who rose from a humble station to the post of minister to the Count of Provence, Raymond Berengar. Romèo served his lord exceedingly well but was defamed by jealous courtiers and subsequently driven to a life of exile and privation in his old age.

Commentary

The chief purpose of Justinian's discourse is to expound upon the sanctity of the empire as a prominent feature of God's plan for human society. Justinian, as an emperor confirmed in the Christian faith, was not only well qualified to establish the great Roman code of secular law but also to assert the eternal role of the empire.

Justinian recognizes that the main facts of Roman history are familiar to Dante. Note how often he introduces an episode with "You know that. . . ." Similarly Dante, in composing the passage, assumes that his audience is also well versed in the history. The purpose of the discourse is to interpret the facts. For instance, Constantine, in transferring the capital from Rome to Constantinople, was turning the eagle backwards, in a direction contrary to that initially taken by Aeneas in moving from Troy to Italy. The significance of Rome as the capital of the empire is all-important in Dante's thinking.

Certain details in the historical sketch may require explanation for readers of our generation. In the opening lines of the canto, the man "who took Lavinia to wife" was Aeneas. The mention of three who fought against three refers to the duel of the Horatii, three brothers defending Rome, versus the Curiatii, three champions of Alba. The "hill beneath which you were born" is the hill just north of Florence on which Fiesole is situated. It was captured by the Romans when Cataline took refuge there. The Rhine, Seine, Rubicon, Spain, Pharsalia, and several other places are cited because of their association with the campaigns of Julius Caesar. The establishment of a (brief) period of world peace under Augustus is symbolized by the closing of the temple of Janus. The crucifixion of Christ, which occurred in the reign of Tiberius, is declared a noble act of vengeance. Then the subsequent destruction of Jerusalem under the Emperor Titus is described as a fitting vengeance against that vengeance. The apparent conflict or contradiction of terms introduced here is not explained until the following canto.

The historical survey of the "everlasting empire" prepares the reader for Dante's warning of present threats to the empire. While the Ghibellines are asserting their proprietary claim to the eagle for their emblem, the Guelfs are attempting to supplant the emblem of the eagle with the French fleur-de-lis. A leader of the movement, "the new

Charles," was Charles II of Apulia, a son of the famous Charles of Anjou (*Purg.* 20).

The souls in the Sphere of Mercury, Dante is informed, devoted their lives to honor and glory, aims which in themselves are laudable, but they allowed their ambitions to overshadow their devotion to the worship of their creator. The only individual introduced from this host of spirits, other than Justinian, is the politician Romèo, about whom a legend had been circulated which Dante accepted. As minister to Raymond Berengar, Romèo had succeeded in arranging marriages with kings for all of the count's four daughters. The circumstances of his undeserved dismissal and the miserable conditions of his exile obviously struck a sympathetic chord for Dante because of his own troubled life in exile.

CANTO 7

Summary

Justinian's spirit, singing praises to God, rejoins the other lights, who appear to be swiftly dancing sparks. Dante stands pondering over a question that Justinian's discourse has raised in his mind but left unanswered, and he yearns to ask Beatrice for an answer but hesitates because of his great reverence for her. She, knowing his unspoken thoughts, offers to expound the complex matter. He fails to understand how one act of vengeance that is just deserves punishment through another act of vengeance. In other words, if the Crucifixion was a just vengeance for Adam's sin, why was it just that Jerusalem should be destroyed in an act of vengeance? To understand the first vengeance, Beatrice declares, one must remember that through Adam's original sin all of his seed were condemned and all men suffered under that sentence until Christ came to earth assuming the nature of man, and so the punishment of Christ (as man) was justified to atone for Adam's sin inasmuch as it was an act against the human side of His nature. At the same time, however, His executioners were committing an act of sacrilege against the divine side of His nature; hence the vengeance which Titus worked against the Jews in destroying Jerusalem was due punishment for that sacrilege.

A second problem puzzling Dante which Beatrice anticipates and expounds is why God chose this particular mode of redemption for mankind. God in his bounty, Beatrice explains, creates objects and beings pure, free from all taint. Such purity was in man's soul when it was created, but its perfection was soiled by Adam's sin. The soul's redemption could only be achieved either through man's atoning or through divine mercy. Divine mercy was revealed when Christ offered Himself as a sacrifice, and atonement was performed through the crucifixion of Christ, the man.

One further aspect of those matters treated by Justinian requires the illumination of Beatrice. We detect in earthly objects the workings of corruption and the brief span of endurance. How can this be reconciled with what was said about the perfection of God's creations? Beatrice explains that what God Himself creates, such as angels and the heavenly bodies, is incorruptible; but earthly elements and objects formed from those elements are created by secondary powers—"informing powers" that reside in the stars. This rule of corruption, then, applies to plants and beasts; but man is of God's own creation, both body and soul, and therefore incorruptible. Remembering that God breathed life into human flesh in Adam and Eve confirms the incorruptibility of man's body as well as his soul, and in this we find justification for the doctrine of the resurrection of body and soul at Judgment Day.

Commentary

In the present canto, which concludes the account of the Sphere of Mercury, the author, through Beatrice, presents solutions to serious problems which arose as a result of the discourse of Justinian, spokesman for the spirits of the region. This passage revealing Dante's confusion and Beatrice's instruction follows the pattern of treatment established in the previous sphere and generally followed through the poem: first, a description of the new scene with its cluster of glowing spirits; then, an introduction of one of the spirits, who converses with the poet, discussing the nature of the sphere and the characters assembled there, and identifying one or more of the spirits of the group; finally, the conversation ended, a discussion with Beatrice to resolve questions left unanswered through the encounter. The questions, as we shall see, are sometimes concerned with astronomy or physics but more frequently with philosophy or theology. In this passage the answers offered by Beatrice are expressed in terms sufficiently clear—if somewhat scholastic in subtlety—so that they scarcely need repeating here.

The reader may find it strange that after listening to Justinian's historical treatise, the main purpose of which was the glorification of the empire, Dante's thoughts should be absorbed with problems centered on redemption. The explanation for this may be that all of the issues raised in the emperor's discourse were resolved except for the seeming paradox of the two vengeances, hence the detailed explanations revolving around that issue.

The role of Beatrice as all-knowing lecturer does her much credit and conforms to her allegorical representation of Divine Wisdom or Revelation, but it is not calculated to endear her to the reader in a personal way. To confirm her in the role of Dante's beloved, the poet introduces many striking passages praising her beauty and her tenderness toward him. One such passage occurs early in this canto:

> Beatrice suffered me to stand thus a little,
> And then, beaming on me with a smile
> Such as would make a man in the fire happy, . . .

CANTO 8

Summary

The planet in the third heavenly sphere, called the Sphere of Venus, was thought by the ancient pagans to be the propagator of love-madness, but in this belief they erred, Dante declares.

The poet, seeing Beatrice become more lovely, suddenly becomes aware of their arrival in a new sphere. He now perceives within the bright light of the planet separate lights like sparks or torches circling as in a dance. Those lights approach swiftly, singing *Hosanna* in such beautiful tones that Dante has longed ever since to hear that sound again.

One spirit, advancing before the rest, declares that all here are prepared to give Dante pleasure, as well as the angelic spirits of the sphere whom Dante addressed in one of his early poems, *"Voi ch' ntendendo il terzo ciel movete"* ("Ye who by intelligence move the Third Heaven"). Dante, much moved, asks the spirit who he is. The speaker replies that Dante loved him on earth and that, had his life not been cut short, much evil might have been avoided. Then without giving his name (Charles Martel), he identifies himself by saying that he had the rule of the Danube region below the German borders and that he should have become lord of the land on the left bank of the Rhone as well as ruler of southern Italy. His heirs would still be ruling in Sicily had it not been for a rebellion brought on by his family's ruthless government. Later, the excessive parsimony of his brother ruling in Naples and the greed of the Spanish troops that served him brought further disaster to the family.

Dante expresses great pleasure in recognizing a former beloved acquaintance and gratification in finding that his noble friend has attained Paradise. Then, pursuing the thought of how different Charles' miserly brother was from their liberal father, he asks Charles to explain why it is that sons do not always inherit the virtues of their parents.

Charles explains how God has ordained that power to exert influence over individual characters shall be vested in the celestial bodies, and that these influences, however differing from one another, are right and in accord with the universal scheme. If God's influence of the heavens were to be imperfect, subject to error, that would imply a possible fault in the Creator. Charles then points out that in a society there must be diversity of characters for the various trades and offices; hence one is born a judge, one a general, one a mechanic. The circling planets imprint characteristics on man's nature in such fashion that Esau differed from his twin brother, Jacob, and a noble son like Romulus was the product of a base father. These apparent irregularities in families are thus to be attributed to Providence (the stars). When it occurs that the dispositions of Providence are overturned by men, as when one born for the sword is made a leader of the Church or when one who is apt for the pulpit is crowned a king, then it is bad for society.

Commentary

The eighth and ninth cantos are devoted to encounters in the Sphere of Venus where Dante meets spirits assigned there because of their too great devotion to a love that was primarily earthly. Oddly enough, however, the eighth canto does not appear to be primarily concerned with the subject of love but rather with problems of heredity.

The opening lines reject the belief of the ancient pagans that the third planet (Venus) drove men into love-madness and degeneracy. The remainder of the canto is concerned more or less directly with the refutation of that belief. The reference to Venus as the planet that woos the sun sometimes from the front, sometimes behind, points to the fact that Venus is sometimes the morning star, sometimes the evening star.

The spirit that comes forward first to greet Dante is Charles Martel, son of Charles II of Apulia and grandson of Charles of Anjou, not to be confused with an earlier and more famous Charles Martel, the grand-father of Charlemagne. Dante's Martel was married to a daughter of the Emperor Rudolph I; his brother was Robert, King of Naples, whose mis-rule is referred to. The titles and family connections of Charles are all alluded to by indirect references which the poet assumes would be readily recognized by his contemporaries. The land of Provence is indi-cated as the region on the left bank of the Rhone River below its junc-ture with the Sorgue; Ausonia is the ancient name for southern Italy, the Kingdom of Naples and Apulia. The lands lying along the Danube below the boundaries of Germany refer to Hungary; Trinacria was the Roman designation for Sicily. Had it not been for the misrule of certain members of the Anjou dynasty, Sicily, Charles says, would still be ruled by the seed of Charles (of Anjou) and of Emperor Rudolph, the grand-father and the father-in-law respectively of Charles Martel. The rebel-lion in which the Sicilian populace cried "Death to the French" and overthrew the rule of the House of Anjou occurred in 1282 and has be-come known in history as the "Sicilian Vespers."

The friendly greeting accorded Dante by Charles Martel clearly implies a past acquaintanceship. Charles paid a formal state visit of several weeks to Florence in 1294, at which time Dante had attained a considerable reputation as the leader of a prominent group of poets. It is fair to assume that Dante presented some of his verses to the young king, quite possibly the very poem referred to here, which, coincident-ally, speaks of the "Intelligences of the Third Heaven." The poem ap-peared later as the first canzone of the *Convivio*.

The remark about the miserliness of Robert which contrasted with his father's liberality leads into the discussion of differences of temper-ament often found within a family. Clearly children do not always in-herit the traits of their parents, and brother can differ from brother. Differences in dispositions and aptitudes among men are necessary to the development of society, which needs persons of diverse talents for diverse occupations. The force which governs the assignment of various talents is Providence; that is, the power which exerts its influence through the stars at one's birth. The lengthy discussion of astronomical influences points toward what might be called predestination or de-terminism and suggests a contradiction of the doctrine of free will set forth in *Purgatorio*. The distinction that Dante would draw to admit the efficacy of both Providence and free will is that though a man's tempera-ment is determined by the stars at birth, he is nevertheless endowed with free will to make choices and is therefore responsible for the dis-position he makes of his talents and the control he exercises over his native weaknesses.

Providence endows individuals with diverse capabilities in order to give society generals, justices, artisans, and ministers. It is a calamity for society when a man suited for the cloth becomes a monarch or when a military type becomes pope.

CANTO 9

Summary

Dante, praising Clemence (possibly Charles Martel's wife, possibly his daughter), cites Charles' prediction of ill to befall his family but adds that those wrongs will be effectively chastised.

A second spirit approaches Dante and, like Charles, is happy to give him satisfaction. She identifies herself as Cunizza, who lived in the region between the Rialto and the headwaters of the Piave and the Brenta rivers. She confesses that her character was formed under the influence of Venus, but she declares that here she is not troubled by regrets for her amorous misdeeds. Pointing to another spirit beside her, she predicts that his fame will live for five hundred years; the reader is not informed of the spirit's identity until later.

Cunizza censures the viciousness that prevails among the people of her native district, Treviso, and she predicts future evils that will befall her neighbors. The "waters of Vicenza" will run red with the blood of Padua's soldiers; a cruel tyrant of the region will meet calamity; and a bishop of Feltro will betray a group of Ghibellines from Ferrara who will seek refuge under his protection.

With the departure of Cunizza, another glowing spirit approaches, the one that she had spoken of as a precious jewel whose fame would last through the centuries. Dante asks why the spirit delays answering the question in Dante's mind, since Dante knows that the spirit can read his thoughts. The spirit then gives his name as Folco (Folquet of Marseilles) and indicates his birthplace—in indirect phrasing—as lying on the Mediterranean coast between Spain and Italy. In his early years, he says, he burned with amorous desires, being under the stamp of Venus, as much as did Dido, Phyllis, or Hercules. Now, however, he reports, as did Cunizza, the memory of those wayward years causes him no remorse.

He points to a spirit whom he identifies as Rahab, a harlot of Jericho who was transported to heaven by Christ in the Harrowing of Hell. Her salvation was earned, despite her sinful life, because she aided Joshua in the capture of Jericho. Folco then denounces Florence because it is the source of "that cursed flower" (the florin) which has corrupted churchmen, causing them to devote themselves to profit, to the neglect of the true spirit of Christianity. Soon, however, he declares, Rome will be delivered from that vice.

Commentary

The identity of the lady named Clemence, addressed in the opening of the canto, is in some doubt. It could have been Charles Martel's wife or his daughter, both of that name. The wife was still living in 1300, the date of Dante's supposed journey through Paradise. She died in 1301. The daughter was Queen of France at the time he was writing the *Paradiso*.

The first spirit to converse with the poet in this canto is Cunizza da Romano, a sister of the notorious tyrant Ezzelino, who is referred to simply as "the fiery brand" (cf. *Inf.* 12). She acknowledges having been dominated by "this burning star" — Venus — for she was known for her amorous adventures in her early life. Later she won acclaim for her charities. Her speech dwells chiefly on the wicked inhabitants of her native province of Treviso and predicts numerous miseries to be visited on them in the near future. Treviso lies mainly to the north of Venice, which is here referred to as the Rialto, the chief island of the city. The battle she speaks of in which the blood of the Paduans will stain the river was one in which Can Grande della Scala defeated the Paduan Guelfs outside Vicenza in 1314. The unnamed tyrant whose downfall Cunizza predicts was a lord of Treviso, a city which stands at the juncture of the two rivers named, the Silë and the Cagnano. The final calamity that Cunizza predicts is the heinous betrayal of thirteen Ghibellines of Ferrara by the Bishop of Feltro. All of these events were accomplished facts when Dante was writing, but were naturally treated as predictions, since they were purported to have been spoken in 1300.

Dante next meets Folco (*Folquet* in French), the spirit whose enduring fame Cunizza predicted. He was a troubadour with a reputation for amorous exploits, but in his later years he entered a Cistercian monastery and eventually became a bishop. His reputation is now clouded because of the cruel role he played in the persecution of the Albigensian heretics, but in Dante's day his name was honored through numerous legends extolling his piety.

Folco's designation of his birthplace is given in a roundabout fashion. On the shores of the great valley flooded with water (the Mediterranean Sea) between the Ebro and the Magra (a river in Spain, a river in Italy) and opposite Bugia (a city on the African coast) is discovered to be Marseilles. This circuitous method of identification is a familiar feature of Dante's style, but in this instance there seems to be more than a testing of the reader's acuteness. One gets the impression that the speaker and his audience are looking down on the face of the earth from an exceedingly great height where large features appear greatly reduced.

Folco compares his former obsessive desires to the wantonness of several characters from pagan antiquity. Dido, the daughter of Belus, causes a double breach of fidelity by her passion for Aeneas — her unfaithfulness to her dead husband, Sichaëus, and Aeneas' unfaithfulness to his dead wife, Creusa. The maiden of Rhodope was Phyllis, who fell in love with Demophoön but was abandoned by him. Alcides (Hercules) met his death through his passion for Iole. Folco repeats Cunizza's assertion that there is no remorse for misconduct here. The souls in heaven are wholly absorbed in joy for their present state and in wonder at God's power and mercy.

To strengthen his point that the lowliest sinners may enjoy God's grace, Folco points to a radiant light who was known as Rahab the Harlot. The story of how she concealed Joshua's spies and thus aided in the taking of Jericho is related in 2 Joshua. The subtle remark about "the cursed flower" from Florence that has corrupted the clergy refers to the florin, the gold coin with the stamp of the Florentine lily that was standard currency throughout Europe. Pope Boniface VIII, Folco adds, has put aside his obligation to liberate the Holy Land, and his clergy are concerned only with the pursuit of profit. He predicts that Rome will soon be rid of the degenerate churchmen, a possible forecast of the removal of the papal seat from Rome to Avignon, which was accomplished in 1305.

CANTO 10

Summary

The reader is urged to contemplate the marvels of the universal plan, in which the various circlings of the sun and the planets provide for the changing of the seasons on earth, without which life could not survive. Furthermore, if the revolutions were greater or lesser, the effects on earth would be disastrous.

Dante suddenly becomes aware that he has now entered the Sphere of the Sun, "the greatest minister of nature," one of indescribable brightness. His mind is so filled with the love of God that it eclipses his feeling for Beatrice. Next, he and Beatrice find themselves surrounded by many individual lights forming a circle similar to the corona that sometimes encircles the moon. Three times the crown of lights circles about the voyagers as in a dance, singing a glorious melody. Then one voice from the group speaks out, offering to answer Dante's unspoken question about the identity of those jewels of light in the crown. He first names the one on his right, Albert of Cologne, then names himself, St. Thomas Aquinas, a Dominican friar. As he goes around the circle, he next names Gratian and Peter Lombard. Then he designates several figures by mentioning their achievements without giving their names; one spirit ranked above all others for his supreme wisdom; another expounded the nature of angels; a third proved that the world had not deteriorated since Christian times, a theory used by Augustine. Continuing around the circle, Aquinas then calls by name: Isidore of Seville, "the Venerable Bede," Richard of St. Victor, and Sigier of Brabant. The circle of spirits, like a clock with its twelve figures, again begins to wheel as they resume their singing in exquisite harmony.

Commentary

Dante and Beatrice have traversed the three spheres which constitute the lower division of Paradise, those which fall within the shadow of the earth, and correspondingly the nature of the spirits associated with those spheres partake of some earthly weakness or imperfection. Marking the transition from the lower to the higher division of Paradise, Dante opens the present canto with a tribute to the wonders of the universal plan. That the earth's polar axis is tilted and that the resultant angle between the equator and the ecliptic is precisely calculated to produce the cycle of the seasons are cited as evidence of the perfection of God. Whoever contemplates this scheme must have his mind lifted to renewed reverence for the Creator.

This new heaven is the Sphere of the Sun, the region of spirits distinguished for their wisdom. The location of the sun below Mars, Jupiter, and Saturn and the assignment of the great teachers and theologians to a position below warriors, rulers, and those devoted to contemplation is not the result of value judgments but rather the consequence of Dante's following the Ptolemaic scheme of the heavens, which placed the sun in the fourth sphere. Dante's enthusiasm for this virtue and for the figures represented in this sphere is indicated by the space allotted to the region and the eloquence of his treatment of the subject.

The first spokesman for the region is St. Thomas Aquinas, who was the chief authority for Dante's theological doctrines, as, in fact, he has been for Roman Catholicism up to the present.

Among the twelve jewels of light in the crown surrounding Dante and Beatrice, some are named, but others not named are identified in terms that would assure their recognition by informed readers of Dante's day. The one whose wisdom has never been equalled is Solomon. One described as the authority on the nature and classification of angels is Dionysius the Areopagite. The author whose work Augustine drew upon is Orosius. The trenchant writer who was martyred for "stripping the world's hypocrisies" is Boethius, author of *On the Consolation of Philosophy.*

Among those in the circle who were named by Aquinas were: Albert of Cologne, "Albertus Magnus," who was Aquinas' teacher; Gratian, whose *Decretum* did much to bring ecclesiastical laws and civil laws into conformity; Peter Lombard, who referred to his voluminous *Sententiae* as his "widow's mite." The Isidore mentioned is St. Isidore of Seville, a seventh-century author. The Venerable Bede is the well-known author of the *Ecclesiastical History of the English Nation.* Richard of St. Victor was the author of an important treatise on contemplation. Sigier of Brabant lectured in Paris in Aquinas' time. Aquinas' remark that Sigier "hammered home invidious truths" is paradoxical; Sigier and Aquinas were enemies at the University of Paris in the thirteenth century. Sigier taught truths according to logic; Aquinas, according to Church doctrine.

CANTO 11

Summary

In an introductory passage the poet reflects upon the vanity of men's pursuits on earth, one person devoting his energies to the law, one to medicine, one to the priesthood, others to power, wealth, or carnal pleasures. How trivial all those activities seem when compared to the state which Dante enjoys in heaven with Beatrice.

The crown of heavenly lights again stops its circling, and Aquinas again addresses Dante. He declares that Providence, to insure the perfect marriage of the Church with Christ, appointed two pious leaders — one a man of great heart, the other of keen mind. He then gives a laudatory account of the career of the first of these men, St. Francis of Assisi. He relates how Francis, in his youth, though born of a wealthy family, declared his devotion to a "Lady" (Poverty), the same lady beloved by Christ. Soon he attracted disciples to his cause — Bernard, Giles, and Sylvester, who adopted their leader's practice of going barefoot, dressed in coarse cloth, and girded with a humble cord. When the number of his followers multiplied, his rule and order received the sanction of Pope Innocent III and later confirmation from Honorius III. During the fifth crusade, Francis journeyed to Egypt, where he boldly preached Christianity to the Sultan. His great sanctity was marked by his receiving the stigmata. At his death he left with his followers the injunction to remain faithful to Lady Poverty.

Continuing his discourse, St. Thomas observes that the second of the great leaders, St. Dominic, also offered admirable instructions to his followers, but, sad to tell, many have become obsessed by greed, and now few of the members of his order remain faithful to his rules of life.

Commentary

The present canto and the one following are devoted to two of the greatest medieval religious leaders, St. Francis of Assisi and St. Dominic, and to the orders of friars that they founded. Both orders were founded early in the thirteenth century. As the geniuses of the leaders differed, so did the aims of the two orders differ. The Franciscans were dedicated primarily to poverty and humble, selfless service to the weak and unfortunate; the Dominicans were devoted chiefly to learning. A century after the founding of those orders, Dante notes that many of their members neglect to follow the principles of their leaders and have become lazy or corrupt (a judgment which, incidentally, was strongly seconded by Chaucer in *The Canterbury Tales*). Furthermore, bitter rivalry and animosity had developed between the Franciscans and the Dominicans in Dante's time.

In heaven we find the chief representatives of these orders fraternizing and praising one another. To honor the name of St. Francis, Dante chooses St. Thomas Aquinas, a Dominican; and, later, the life of St. Dominic is related by a distinguished Franciscan, St. Bonaventura.

In the account of the career of St. Francis, Dante, through Aquinas, indicates his birthplace by first naming rivers and towns in the vicinity of Assisi, and in the same fashion he withholds the name of the saint until he is well into the account. Assisi is perched on a hill between two rivers, the Tupino and the Chiascio (where St. Ubaldo had his hermitage), and lies to the north of Perugia. There is a play on the word *Ascesi*, which was the old Tuscan form of Assisi, but which also means "I have risen" and is here referring to the sun and daybreak.

Of the numerous rules of conduct set down by St. Francis for his disciples, Dante emphasizes one, the dedication to a life of poverty, a feature of the life of Francis which invited comparison with the life of Christ, and a guiding principle that Dante believed to be a keystone for the restoration of true Christianity. Similarly Dante selected from the many accounts of miracles in the life of the saint only one to recite, the receiving of the stigmata, which further emphasizes the resemblance of St. Francis to Christ.

The censure of those followers of St. Dominic who have neglected his rule of life is pronounced, it should be noted, by a Dominican.

CANTO 12

Summary

As the circle of lights again starts its wheeling dance, a second circle approaches and surrounds the first, moving in unison and singing in rapturous harmony with it. A voice from one of the lights in the new circle addresses Dante, saying that it is impelled to extol the greatness of St. Dominic, since he and St. Francis strove together in a common cause. When Christians had strayed from the path, Christ appointed those two men as champions to succor His bride and lead the stragglers back to the true path.

In a land to the west, beyond which the sun sets for all men, in Calahorra, which is under the ensign of two lions, was born this champion of the faith. His mother had a prophetic dream of his greatness before his birth, and his godmother was also visited by a favoring dream before his baptism. He was named Dominic, "of the Lord." In his infancy he was often found by his nurse awake upon the ground, looking as if he would say, "For this end am I come." It was no accident that his father was named Felix (happy) and his mother Giovanna (the grace of God). As Christ's minister he held to the Master's chief counsels. Early he became renowned as a brilliant teacher, and he traveled widely preaching his message. When he appealed to papal authority, it was not for personal profit or advancement but for sanction to combat the doctrines of the heretics; and he struck his best blows where resistance was most stubborn. In his long career he did much to cultivate the "Catholic garden," the fruits of which have prospered ever since.

The speaker next reverts to St. Francis, the comrade with St. Dominic in the struggle to restore the true Christian life. He complains that now many of the followers of Francis have turned from the path of their leader, either neglecting or twisting the interpretation of the rules. There are still a few who are faithful, but leaders of contending factions, one from Casale and one from Acquasparta, are causing a grievous division in the ranks of the order.

The speaker now announces that he is Bonaventura (a Franciscan). He names the spirits in the second circle of shining lights. The first two, Illuminato and Austen (Agostino), were among the early converts of St. Francis. Others named around the circle are: Hugh of St. Victor, Peter Mangiadore, Peter of Spain, Nathan the Prophet, St. John Chrysostom, St. Anselm, Donatus, Rabanus, and Joachim the Calabrian abbot.

Bonaventura repeats that his eulogy for St. Dominic is a response to the generous praise accorded St. Francis by Aquinas.

Commentary

The appearance of the second circle of spirits, its conformity to the motion of the first circle, and the harmonious choiring of the two are symbolic of the harmony that reigns among the various religious orders in heaven.

St. Bonaventura, who acts as spokesman for the newly arrived spirits, was appointed General of the Franciscan Order and was the author of a work on the life of St. Francis. His account of St. Dominic's career obviously counterpoints that of St. Francis, reported by Aquinas. That Dominic was ordained by heaven for his great mission was revealed by his mother's vision before his birth. It is reported that she dreamed she gave birth to a dog with a flaming torch in its mouth. The godmother's dream was of a baby with a bright star shining in his forehead.

Dominic's birthplace is revealed through references to a western land (Spain), the city of Callaroga (or Calahorra) in old Castile, which

is indicated by the reference to its coat of arms: a shield quartered with
two lions and two castles, one lion above a castle and one beneath the
other castle. The saint's religious aims are contrasted with the worldly
goals of "him of Ostia" and Thaddeus. The former, Enrico of Susa, was
typical of the scholars devoted to studying the *Decretals* (canon law);
the latter, a physician bent on serving for profit. Dominic did not apply
for permission to withhold part of the money due for charity ("for leave
to dispense two or three for six"), as many clergy did; nor did he seek
benefices. His one request was for permission to combat heresy. The
remark "where opposition was most stubborn" appears to be a reference
to his mission in Provence preaching against the Albigensian heresy.
Bonaventura's concluding observation that from the saint sprang
"streams that watered the garden of the Church" is more than justified
by the great services of the Dominicans in educational and intellectual
fields.

The bitter commentary delivered by Bonaventura on the quarrel-
ing factions within the Franciscan order matches the complaint of
Aquinas over the defection of his fellow Dominicans. The citation of
the schools of Casale and Acquasparta has reference to factions within
the Franciscan order known as "the Spiritualists," led by Ubertino of
Casale, and "the Conventuals," headed by Matteo of Acquasparta, who
advocated relaxing the old rules.

The lights of the second ring, who are named by Bonaventura, are
as follows: Illuminato and Agostino, early converts to the teachings of
St. Francis; Hugh of St. Victor, a famous theologian of Paris; Peter Mangiadore of Troyes and later of St. Victor in Paris; Peter of Spain, who
became Pope John XXI; Nathan, the Old Testament character who rebuked David (II Samuel, 12); St. Chrysostom, who was made patriarch
of Constantinople; St. Anselm, an archbishop of Canterbury; Donatus,
a famous Roman grammarian; Rabanus, an archbishop of Mayence and
a prominent theologian; and Joachim of Flora, an abbot of Calabria
who propounded the theory of the coming dispensation of the Holy
Ghost.

CANTO 13

Summary

In attempting to convey an impression of the brilliance of those
spinning circles of light, Dante tells the reader to imagine twenty-four
of the brightest stars he knows—including the Great and Little Dippers

—and imagine them arranged as a double crown; then realize that that image would be exceeded greatly by the lights that surround him and Beatrice. The circles are wheeling in opposite directions in their dance, and all the while they sing of the glory of the Trinity and Christ's dual nature (human and divine).

St. Thomas Aquinas speaks again, offering to resolve one of the problems in Dante's mind concerning the superior wisdom of Solomon. How can it be that Solomon has had no equal for wisdom? Dante believes that both Adam and Christ were endowed with perfect wisdom, hence would be placed above Solomon. The complex explanation involves a restatement of the differences between those beings created directly by God and those created by God's ministers, "the nine contingencies (or subsistences)." The former, God's original creations, include the angels and also Adam and Christ (in His human aspect); they are naturally exempted from the comparison with Solomon. When God asked Solomon what gift he desired, Solomon asked for wisdom to rule well; consequently, Solomon's wisdom is the subject of comparison with the wisdom of other earthly rulers.

Aquinas concludes his discourse with an admonition against making uninformed judgments and coming to hasty conclusions. To illustrate such errors, he cites certain misguided philosophers, Parmenides, etc., and heretical teachers, such as Arius and Sabellius.

Commentary

The discourse resumed at this point by Aquinas is concerned with a remark that he made earlier which puzzled Dante — namely, that Solomon's wisdom was never equalled by another human being. The explanation given involves a distinction between those beings created by God and those created by His agents, the basis for exempting Christ and Adam from comparison with other men. This discussion relates to the theory regarding the cause of imperfections and individual differences among men that was propounded by Charles Martel in the Sphere of Venus (Canto 8).

The basis for the high regard for Solomon's wisdom is the biblical passage relating a dream of Solomon in which the Lord appeared to him and asked what gift he would choose. Solomon's answer was: ". . . an understanding heart to judge Thy people, that I may discern between good and bad. . . ." The Lord was pleased with his choice and replied: ". . . I have given thee a wise and understanding heart; so that there was none like thee before thee, neither after thee shall any arise like unto thee" (I Kings, 3).

In his parting words of counsel to Dante, Aquinas cautions him against making hasty conclusions or building up systems upon misinformation or insufficient evidence. Among those cited for faulty judgment are early philosophers who were criticized by Aristotle — Parmenides, Melissus, and Bryson — and promoters of heretical doctrines — Sabellius and Arius. This speech of admonition (112-142), though neither profound nor original, is surely appropriate to the Sphere of the Sun. Furthermore, it is elevated by the introduction of several striking figurative passages.

CANTO 14

Summary

Beatrice speaks to the angelic spirits asking for a clarification of one more problem in Dante's mind. The question is whether or not the souls will retain their present brilliance after the Resurrection, when the bodies will be joined to their souls; and if such brightness will remain, how the eyes will endure it? The spirits join in singing a hymn to the Trinity three times, and then a voice from one of the spirits in the inner circle (Solomon) offers an explanation. The souls will indeed retain their brilliance, which is an outward expression of their ardor. The eyes, and all the organs of the body, will grow in strength to endure that excessive brightness. The final reunion of body and soul is destined to restore the individual's completeness in the final stage of everlasting glory.

A third ring of lights appears and takes its place surrounding the other circles, and it intensifies in brightness until Dante has to lower his gaze. Beatrice restores Dante's confidence with a smile, and when he lifts his glance he discovers that they have entered a new sphere, the Sphere of Mars. He expresses the intense joy he feels in the presence of the ruddy planet by offering a silent prayer to God. Within the new sphere he perceives two enormous beams of light which intersect to form a cross, the symbol for Christ. Within those beams flash many smaller lights, the spirits of this sphere, moving to and fro in the intricate patterns of a dance; as they dance, they sing a marvelous hymn which ravishes Dante's soul although he does not fully comprehend its meaning. He declares that the sweetness of that encounter — the sight of the dancing lights and the beauty of their song — surpassed any pleasure he had yet known. Then, not to detract from the thrilling presence of Beatrice, he explains that he had not yet turned his glance to her since they arrived in this sphere.

Commentary

The problem under discussion here has to do with the doctrine that our bodies will be joined to our souls at the Judgment Day, which was a commonly accepted belief. The argument runs that man was created with a body and a soul and that he will attain perfection in heaven only when body and soul are joined to restore the completeness of the individual. Dante does not question the belief in that reunion, but he wonders how the human body, with its limited sensibilities, will be capable of enduring the brilliant radiance which the souls have acquired in their present heavenly state. Solomon's answer is, of course, that the sensory organs will develop to the point of tolerating the intensified sensations. At the conclusion of Solomon's speech, the spirits all cry "Amen," showing that they look forward with pleasure to the recovery of their bodies.

The appearance of the third circle of lights is treated with surprising brevity. No names are mentioned and no special significance is hinted at in the passage. The best explanation for the introduction of this third, outer circle is that it completes the symbol of the Trinity and that it foreshadows the scene at the climax of Paradise where the vision of God is represented in three circles of dazzling brilliance.

The Sphere of Mars, into which Dante is now transported, is characterized first by its reddish cast of light, for this is known to astronomers as the red planet. His expression of thanks to God, "a burnt offering in the language common to all," means simply a silent prayer. The sign of this sphere is a cross, a familiar symbol for Christ and also for the crusaders who populate the sphere, soldiers of the cross. The great beams forming the cross are likened to the Milky Way. Here the dance of the spirits and the harmony of their singing are more glorious than any sights and sounds Dante has yet encountered; for, as he explains, each higher stage of heaven intensifies the beauty and brilliance of its spirits. Correspondingly, Beatrice appears more luminous at each advancing state of the journey and inspires in Dante a more thrilling joy.

CANTO 15

Summary

The music stops, as if by command, and a light from the right arm of the cross descends to its foot, blazing like a shooting star. The spirit in the light welcomes Dante to the sphere, calling him one "of my own blood" and praising him for the gift of grace that has permitted him to journey through Paradise while still alive. After speaking for a time of things too profound for Dante's comprehension, he tells Dante that he has been eagerly awaiting his coming, of which he read in the Book of Fate. He urges Dante to utter the questions that are in his mind, for even though the spirits can read those unexpressed thoughts, it will be pleasing for him to hear them voiced by Dante. In Dante's response, he apologizes for not being capable of expressing adequately in words his gratitude for the paternal greeting of the spirit, and he humbly asks the spirit's name. The spirit answers that his son was Dante's great-grandfather, the ancestor from whom Dante's family derived its name.

Florence, the spirit tells Dante, was in his lifetime a city of peace, sobriety, and modesty. She shunned the use of showy adornments; she had no ostentatious mansions and her customs did not admit lascivious indulgences. She had not come to the point of surpassing Rome in splendor. Men went in plain dress and women did not paint their faces but attended to their household duties faithfully. He tells how fortunate he was to be born at such a time in such a city. In the city's ancient baptistry, he was christened Cacciaguida. His wife, who came from the valley of the Po, brought the surname of Alighiero into the family. Cacciaguida joined the Emperor Conrad III on a crusade and was knighted by him for good service. He died in battle against the Saracens and was thus martyred and transported to "this peace."

Commentary

The crusader who first addresses Dante in the Sphere of Mars is introduced with considerable fanfare. Evidently the poet wishes to make his entrance impressive. He is Cacciaguida, Dante's great-great-grandfather. His first words, spoken in Latin, claim a blood relationship and express his delight at Dante's arrival and his admiration for the special grace bestowed on the poet. Altogether his reception of Dante is exceedingly cordial, and Dante's reply is humble and grateful.

Cacciaguida says that his son, Alighiero, the family namesake, has been on the Terrace of Pride in Purgatory for a hundred years and that

Dante would do well to offer prayers for some remission of his further penalty.

Cacciaguida then delivers a lengthy eulogy to the Florence of the twelfth century, when the citizens lived simple, virtuous lives. Corruption and excesses of luxury had not become prevalent. The portrait he draws of that earlier way of life is similar to accounts of life among the Romans in the early days of the Republic or of life in colonial America. It is obviously intended to serve as a contrast to what Florence had become in Dante's time.

CANTO 16

Summary

Dante observes that it is not surprising if men on earth pride themselves on nobility of birth, because even in heaven he was infected with that same kind of pride as he talked with his noble ancestor. He now recognizes that nobility of blood is something that quickly diminishes unless it is constantly renewed and strengthened.

He humbly begs Cacciaguida to tell him when he lived, who his ancestors were, and what worthy families were in Florence in his time. The elder indicates the date of his birth by saying that this planet (Mars) had made 553 revolutions since the Annunciation of Christ's birth, which tells us that he was born about 1100 A.D. He designates the neighborhood where his family lived but prefers not to give further information about his forebears. The population of Florence then, he says, was only one-fifth of its present population, not having yet been swollen by inroads from surrounding villages and farms. Had it not been for the conspiring of the Church against the Empire, Florence would not have become involved in capturing towns in Tuscany, victories which flooded Florence with refugees.

Since cities rise and fall, says Cacciaguida, it should be no matter for surprise that families follow the same pattern, even as the tides ebb and flow. He then recites a long list of families that were prominent in his day but have lost their distinction by Dante's time, noting in certain instances the causes for dissension among feuding families or parties.

Commentary

Dante's philosophical observations regarding the fallacy of taking pride in the nobility of blood repeats a sentiment that he expressed on earlier occasions (the third *canzone* of *Convivo* and in *Purg.* 11). By addressing Cacciaguida with the plural form *voi*, a mark of dignified formality, Dante gives Beatrice a clue to his feelings about his distinguished ancestry, at which she shows him by her smile her awareness of his weakness.

In response to Dante's questioning, Cacciaguida continues his account of Florence as he knew it two centuries earlier. The way he indicates the date of his birth has led to a variety of interpretations. In the first place, there is a difference in the reading of manuscripts and early texts, some using the figure 553 (550 and 3), some using 580 (550 and 30). Then, too, there is the debate over whether the time for the circuit of Mars' orbit should be computed roughly as two years or more precisely as 687 days. Different commentators have dated his birth between 1090 and 1106.

Since Cacciaguida's day the city's population has increased, but the character of its citizens has degenerated through the influx of country folk and people from the outlying villages that have come under Florentine domination. Much of the trouble has stemmed from the interference of the Church ("the people most degenerate in all the world") against the authority of the Empire (Caesar). He cites the names of numerous leading families of his time that are now of slight consequence, most of them names carrying no meaning or interest for modern readers but surely holding more interest for Dante's contemporaries. Among the families mentioned that have risen to prominence since those early days, a few deserve special notice because they move in and out of the scenes in Florentine history. The Buondelmonti and the Amidei developed a bitter feud over a jilted bride that led to the Guelf-Ghibelline split among the Florentines. The Cerchi tribe, immigrants from Pistoia, became leaders of the Whites in a second intra-city feud.

CANTO 17

Summary

Encouraged by Beatrice, Dante asks his ancestor to tell him what the misfortunes are that have been intimated to him by several of the spirits he has talked to on his journey. Cacciaguida first explains that events of the future are seen in the mind of God, as in a mirror, but do not interfere with man's free will. He then proceeds to relate the imminent exile of Dante from Florence, the outcome of a plot involving the pope. He forecasts the privations, humiliation, and isolation in store for the poet in his wandering among strangers, and how, after becoming disappointed with his fellow exiles, he will break with them and take his own way, literally and figuratively.

Dante's first true refuge, Cacciaguida tells him, will be with a Lombard (Bartolommeo della Scala, of Verona) whose family crest shows an eagle above a ladder. Della Scala will receive him with honor and anticipate his needs and desires. At della Scala's court Dante will meet a youth of exceeding promise whose later deeds will win him great renown (Can Grande della Scala). What great deeds he will perform are related to Dante but he is instructed not to report them in advance.

As Cacciaguida concludes his moving forecast of Dante's future calamities, he promises that the poet will live to witness the avenging of the perfidies of those Florentines who will sentence him.

Dante believes the warning he has received will aid him in facing the approaching trials. He then asks pointedly if it will be wise for him to reveal all that he has learned on his journey when he returns to earth, considering how many persons would be embittered by things he could tell. He recognizes that, on the other hand, by timidly withholding the truth he will lose credit with future generations ("those who will call these times ancient"). Cacciaguida urges him to "make his whole vision manifest," no matter who is displeased by it: "Let them scratch where it itches." If Dante's words at first seem harsh, Cacciaguida says, they will nevertheless provide good nourishment for those who will digest them; it was for this that Dante was conducted through these regions, where he was shown chiefly persons of renown in order that his hearers might be more impressed by what he has to report than they would be with accounts of humble individuals.

Commentary

It has been made clear earlier in the narrative that the spirits of the dead can foretell future events, a fact which might lead us to suppose that all our actions are foreordained. Cacciaguida denies this supposition categorically, stating that God's foreknowledge does not rule our acts.

Since Dante has heard indefinite prophecies of misfortunes that are in store for him, he urges his great ancestor to tell him more precisely what he may expect so that he can prepare himself for those misfortunes. The prophecy given by Cacciaguida of Dante's exile and the resulting misery and degradation was written, as we know, after Dante had experienced twelve or fifteen years of wandering in exile. Though written in simple, quiet language, it is one of the most moving and memorable passages in the *Comedy*. Dante's relationship with the Whites who were exiled at the same time is indicated only briefly. Contemporary records confirm the fact that he joined with other Florentine outcasts for a time, but they give us no certain explanation for his break with them. Certainly, by deciding to go his own way he could maintain his integrity, but at the same time he increased the loneliness of his wanderings.

In identifying the della Scala family, Dante paid grateful tribute to one of his best patrons. There is more in his relations with them than appreciation for shelter and kindness; there is also the link with his life-long hope for the restoration of imperial rule in Italy, which was centered in part on Henry VII and in part on Can Grande della Scala (cf. notes to *Inf.* 1 and *Purg.* 33), the member of the family referred to by Cacciaguida as a youth who was destined to perform great deeds.

One last point on which Dante wishes to consult his honored ancestor is the question of whether or not he ought to relate everything he has seen and heard on his journey when he returns to his earthly life. He faces the choice of stirring up great bitterness among certain of his contemporaries or losing the respect of posterity. In that speech he reveals his hopes that "his fame will live on through his book." The sentiment is similar to that expressed by Brunetto Latini (*Inf.* 15). Cacciaguida's reply amounts to a command to Dante to reveal all his experiences for the profit of those who will hear and digest them. It is to be noted that the word "vision" is here used to refer to Dante's journey.

CANTO 18

Summary

While Cacciaguida appears to be absorbed with his own reflections, Dante looks toward Beatrice and finds in her eyes such a shining expression of love that he doubts his power to describe it. His gaze is soon interrupted, however, by Beatrice, who notices Cacciaguida's changed expression and directs Dante's attention back to him.

Cacciaguida declares that it would not be proper for Dante to leave the Sphere of Mars without being shown some of the great soldiers who shine in the cross. He names Joshua, Judas Maccabaeus, Charlemagne, Roland, William of Orange, Renouard, Godfrey of Bouillon, and Robert Guiscard; and as each hero is named, his light gleams with added brightness and stirs with additional motion.

Turning his gaze again to Beatrice, Dante observes her features becoming ever brighter; whereupon he realizes that they have been transported into a new sphere. The light around them is white, in contrast to the reddish cast in Mars, a sign to Dante that they have arrived at the "temperate star," Jupiter.

The lights of the souls here, soaring and wheeling like a great flock of birds, change their formations to spell the letters of a message: first *D*, then *I*, then *L*, and so on. The full message reads DILIGITE IUSTITIAM QUI IUDICATIS TERRAM ("love justice, ye that judge the earth"). At the end of the message the *M* remains. Soon new lights come to rest above it, and the figure of the *M* is transformed, first to the emblem of the lily, and then finally to complete the figure of an eagle.

In an apostrophe to the planet, Dante declares how he came to understand that justice on earth is the reflection of heavenly justice. He then inveighs against the papacy, which ought to be the seat of earthly justice but which instead has come to be the mercenary perverter of justice through abuses of excommunication. He concludes with a warning to the reigning pope, who has replaced the ideals of Peter and Paul with the image of John the Baptist (imprinted on the florin) as the object of his devotion.

Commentary

Dante's recording of his apprehension of Beatrice's increasing beauty and of his mounting joy in her company is one of the most effective devices he employs to register the ascending scale of the glories he is witnessing and the soaring of his feelings.

Several of the great warriors who are pointed out to Dante are well known to every reader — Joshua, Charlemagne, and Roland — but others are less universally recognized. Judas Maccabaeus was a general who led the Jewish army against Syria in the second century B.C. His deeds are recorded in the Vulgate Bible. William of Orange — not to be confused with later figures in the history of the Netherlands and England — was a ninth-century French hero who fought against the Saracens in southern France. Rainouart was a converted Saracen who fought with

William. Godfrey of Bouillon was commander-in-chief of the First Crusade. Robert Guiscard was the leader who established Norman rule in Sicily and Southern Italy in the eleventh century by defeating the Saracens there.

Upon arrival in the sixth heavenly sphere, Jupiter, Dante is greeted with a new series of figured formations that spell out, letter by letter, a scriptural message. The literal English translation is "Love justice, ye who judge the earth."

Before completing the description of the emblem formed by the lights of Jupiter, the poet invokes one of the muses for aid in setting forth worthily what he saw there. He does not name the muse but he uses the term "Pegasean divinity," suggesting Pegasus, the winged horse associated with the muses. It is generally assumed that he was invoking Calliope, the Greek muse of epic poetry.

The step-by-step transformation of the final M into an eagle introduces a series of symbolic renderings. M signifies monarchy. The eagle was the emblem of Rome and, consequently, stands for imperial unity and dominion. The figure of the lily, an intermediate stage in the transformation of the M into the eagle, is presumably the emblem of Florence and its ruling Guelf party, the suggestion being that the Guelfs must eventually yield to the ideal of a unified empire.

The invectives pronounced against the papacy may be taken, in general, as directed against several of the recent popes. It is their "smoke" that has dimmed the beams of Jupiter through their "buying and selling in the temple." The attack, however, becomes more directly personal with the charge of withholding the bread of mercy—a reference to the abuse of recommunications. The particular object of this attack was Pope John XXII, who was accused of excommunicating numbers of people in order to collect heavy fees for their reinstatement. Here Dante has left the pretense that he is speaking in 1300 about affairs as they stood at that time. John XXII's papacy lasted from 1316 until 1334, the period in which this passage was composed.

The allusion to Peter and Paul, with their examples of miracles and martyrdom, are clear enough, but in the suggestion that the incumbent pope is more devoted to John the Baptist lies the implication that he is greedy for money. Here, as on several other occasions, the poet has let the figure of the Baptist symbolize the love of money because of his image on the florin.

CANTO 19

Summary

The many spirits making up the great emblem of the eagle, each one shining like a brilliant ruby, address Dante, all speaking in unison and using the pronouns "I" and "my" as if one spirit spoke, the voice of justice. It first declares that it has left a name on earth for justice and piety. Then Dante begs for some clarification of the mysteries of divine justice, which he could never learn on earth. The eagle responds by saying that creation is of such infinite complexity that not even the highest of the created beings, the archangel Lucifer, could comprehend it. It follows that the lesser beings cannot hope to comprehend even the finite portion of creation that concerns them. Man's understanding can no more read the riddles of the universe than can his vision penetrate the depths of the ocean.

The eagle detects a question distressing Dante; that is, where is the justice of condemning a native of India who has never heard of Christ and who is therefore denied a place in Paradise, even though he has led a blameless life? The answer is that for such inscrutable questions man's only recourse is to accept the authority of the Scriptures.

In further speech the eagle declares that on Judgment Day those who did not know Christ may be closer to Him than some who proclaim themselves Christians but commit heinous sins. It then denounces numerous sovereigns whose crimes will bring them to damnation when the recording angel reads the records of their acts.

Commentary

Each spirit in the emblem shines with its own light, and yet all speak in unison as a demonstration of the unity of justice. The voice of the eagle declares that man cannot expect to grasp the complex scope of the plan of the Creator, hence can little fathom the workings of divine justice. He therefore must put his faith in the word of the Bible. Dante is, nevertheless, consumed with desire to understand why virtuous heathens must be denied the blessings awarded to good Christians. This is an echo of the concern he expressed upon meeting the noble spirits of antiquity in Limbo (*Inf.* 4). The eagle responds, like the Voice out of the Whirlwind addressing Job, with a question: "Who are you to judge such a case, you who are so limited in view?" One does best to trust in authority and, above all, remember that whatever is good comes from God and that nothing that comes from God can be evil.

The voice of the eagle further explains that virtuous heathens will be closer to Christ on Judgment Day than many professed Christians. By way of examples, it names contemporary or near contemporary rulers and potentates, all of whom were guilty of crimes unworthy of their noble stations. The Emperor Albert of Austria is blamed for his invasion of Prague's kingdom (Bohemia); Philip IV, "the Fair," who was killed by a wild boar, is blamed for his corruption of French currency; Edward I of England and the Scottish Wallace, for their border feuds; Ferdinand IV of Castile and Wenceslas IV of Bohemia for their vicious lives; and Charles II of Naples, the titular King of Jerusalem, who neglected his responsibility to lead a crusade and restore the Holy City to Christian rule. His good deeds are marked with *1*, his errant deeds with *M*, the Roman numeral for 1,000. Other renegade rulers mentioned nearly complete the list of living sovereigns: Frederick II of Sicily; his uncle, King of the Balearic Islands; and Frederick's brother, King of Aragon; Dionysius of Portugal; Haakon of Norway; Stephen of Rascia, who counterfeited Venetian coins; and Henry II of Lusignano, who kept the French reign over Cyprus (Nicosia and Famagusta, cities on Cyprus).

CANTO 20

Summary

After an interval of exquisite song, the eagle resumes its discourse with Dante, pointing out that the noblest of the souls in that emblem form its eye. At the very center, the pupil of the eye, stands David, the author of the Psalms and the king who brought the Ark of the Covenant back to Jerusalem. Above the pupil are five other lights forming the eyebrow, identified as the Emperor Trajan; Hezekiah, a King of the Jews; the Emperor Constantine; William II of Sicily; and Ripheus, a Trojan hero.

Dante is so surprised at learning that certain of these personages are included in this honored company that he blurts out a question: "How can this be?" The eagle recognizes that Dante's confusion concerns two of the figures who he supposed were pagans, Trajan and Ripheus. Trajan, the eagle explains, was brought back to life from Limbo through the intercession of St. Gregory's prayers so that he might be converted to the faith and die a second time a Christian. The case of Ripheus is perhaps even stranger. He was granted the foreknowledge of Christ's coming to earth and suffering for mankind; and, believing, he was baptized through the ministrations of those three ladies of the three Christian virtues, faith, hope, and love.

The eagle concludes its discourse with an admonition to mortals to refrain from hasty judgments, considering that not even the souls in heaven know what souls are among the elect. At the conclusion of the meeting, the two souls in question, Trajan and Ripheus, intensify in brightness as a sign of their pleasure.

Commentary

As a counterpart to the list of reprobate monarchs given in the preceding canto, Dante now offers a list of some of the noblest spirits among the lights of Jupiter. The identifications of these personages given by the eagle are indirect in most instances, only two of them being called by name. The "singer of the Holy Ghost" who brought the Ark from house to house is, of course, King David. The ruler who consoled the poor widow for her son is Trajan, the emperor whose act of humility was depicted in *Purgatorio* among the "goads" on the Terrace of Pride *(Purg.* 10). Though Trajan lived after the time of Christ, he was not a Christian during his natural lifetime; but, according to a legend, he was later redeemed, having been granted a special dispensation through the prayers of St. Gregory (Pope Gregory I, known familiarly as Gregory the Great).

The next to be mentioned, the Hebrew king who, through his own prayers, was allowed to delay his death long enough to rectify his way of life, is Hezekiah. The incident is related in II Kings, 20. The ruler who "became a Greek," that is, who transferred the capital of the empire to Constantinople, was Constantine. His well-intentioned action resulted in evil consequences but Dante condones the "high purpose" of the act, regardless of its consequences.

The only contemporary figure included in this distinguished group is William II, "the Good," of Naples and Sicily, a twelfth-century ruler in that land which now, the Eagle says, mourns under the tyranny of Charles, "the King of Jerusalem," and Frederick II of Sicily, two of those evil modern sovereigns cited in the preceding canto.

The last of those named in this special group, and one who caused Dante's special perplexity, is Ripheus the Trojan, a character who is briefly mentioned in the *Aeneid* as one who loved justice. By representing this ancient pagan as one of the blessed spirits in heaven, Dante is declaring his stand on the much debated question of whether or not baptism is an absolute requirement for attaining paradise. At the same time, he is also illuminating the question of divine justice raised in the preceding canto regarding the chance for salvation of an Indian on the banks of the Ganges who has led a blameless life but who has never heard of Christ.

This canto contains a curious passage of formal rhetorical construction similar to the passage in *Purgatorio* 12 with its repetition of initial words at regular intervals. In the present canto, the six notables are presented in a series of double tercets or six-line passages; and in each instance the second tercet begins with the words *"Ora conosce . . ."* ("Now he knows"). The repeated phrase serves to point up the structural pattern, but it also effectively emphasizes the state of blessedness which is the reward of these virtuous rulers.

CANTO 21

Summary

The scene opens with yet another ecstatic expression of the glory of Beatrice's beauty, a signal that the two have arrived at a new sphere. Beatrice instructs Dante to turn his gaze to this new region which is ruled by Saturn, the god who, according to pagan mythology, reigned over the world in the Golden Age. There Dante discovers a golden ladder mounting upward out of sight; on the ladder, the bright lights of spirits are seen ascending and descending.

When one of the spirits draws near, Dante, encouraged by Beatrice, asks why he has come down the ladder to approach the visitors and also why it is that there is no singing here as there was in each of the spheres below. The spirit's answer to the second question is that the absence of singing is to spare Dante's mortal ears. He says further that he has come down the ladder to greet Dante and to "make him glad." Dante then asks the spirit why he, of all those lights, was elected for this service. At that, the spirit begins to express his ecstasy by spinning around swiftly like a cartwheel and replies that he has been touched by a divine beam from heaven that enables him to contemplate the Supreme Being; but as to the reason for his selection — or predestination — for this role, he cannot fathom it, nor can any created being. He then admonishes Dante to take the message back to earth that men should abstain from attempting to resolve this problem of predestination and other mysteries of creation.

Dante then asks the spirit his name. He announces that he is Peter Damian, and he relates that in his early years he lived a holy life in a monastery on Mt. Catria, but later he was appointed to offices in the active service of the Church, finally attaining the rank of cardinal. He concludes his discourse with a severe censure of the present clergy, who, so unlike St. Peter and St. Paul, have grown exceedingly fat and rich.

Other spinning lights descend the ladder to join Peter Damian and unite in a thunderous shout that robs Dante of his senses.

Commentary

The arrival of Dante and Beatrice in the seventh planetary sphere is marked by the increased radiance of Beatrice, which is such that she dares not smile at Dante lest that would increase her glory to a point beyond the power of Dante's mortal senses.

The Sphere of Saturn is consecrated to the fourth cardinal virtue, temperance. The souls assigned to the region are those devoted to contemplation, which in medieval doctrine was held to be the highest form of Christian virtue. An indication of the prominence given to the contemplative life was shown in *Purgatorio* (Cantos 27, 30-33) in its allegorical representation of the figures of Rachel and Beatrice. A life devoted to contemplation could be achieved only in monastic isolation.

Dante is surprised that there is no singing here, but it should be recognized that quiet surroundings are appropriate for contemplation. A further reason offered for the absence of song is the necessity of sparing Dante's mortal senses, "the same reason that Beatrice has no smile."

As in the lower spheres, each planet has its emblem—the crown for the Sphere of the Sun, the cross for Mars, the eagle for Jupiter—so Saturn has the emblem of the golden ladder. It symbolizes the means for the soul's ascent through divine contemplation. The source for this familiar medieval emblem was the biblical account of Jacob's vision: "Behold a ladder set up on earth, and the top of it reached to heaven, and behold the angels of God ascending and descending on it" (Gen. 28).

The spokesman for the spirits here is Peter Damian, a notable church figure of the eleventh century. Much of his life was passed in a monastery in the Apennines, where he became known as an effective reformer of Church discipline. In his mature years he served as papal legate on several important missions. On one of his missions to the imperial court, he succeeded in persuading the young Emperor Henry

IV to abandon his plan to divorce Bertha of Savoy. At length he was permitted to return to the quiet of monastic life, much to his joy.

Dante, in questioning Peter Damian regarding his selection for this assistance to Dante, is really trying to fathom the puzzle of predestination. The saint not only does not offer an explanation but he urges the poet to take the message back to men on earth that they are not to pry into this inscrutable question.

Damian concludes his discourse with a complaint about the decline of the modern clergy from the models of St. Peter (Cephas) and St. Paul (the Vessel of the Holy Ghost), who went barefoot and lean. *Cephas* is the Aramaic word for *stone*, the equivalent of the Latin *Petrus*.

CANTO 22

Summary

The thunderous roar uttered by the host of spirits fills Dante with fright, whereupon Beatrice explains that it expresses a denunciation of the deterioration of clerical life as designated by Peter Damian and a prayer for the punishment of the offenders.

Another brilliant light from among the spirits on the ladder speaks to Dante; it is St. Benedict, who relates how he brought Christianity to the pagans in the neighborhood of Monte Cassino, where he founded a famous monastery. He then points to two other spirits among the crowd of those devoted to this contemplative life, St. Maccarius and St. Romualdus.

Dante begs for the privilege of seeing Benedict in his bodily form. The saint replies that the request can be gratified only when Dante arrives in the highest heaven. St. Benedict then pronounces a bitter censure of monastic life at present, calling the religious houses dens of thieves. He particularly denounces usury and the misdirection of monies that should be spent for the relief of the poor. None, he declares, now lifts his feet to mount up Jacob's Ladder. Then, having sounded his condemnation of his living followers, he returns to his companion lights who together ascend the golden ladder.

At a sign from Beatrice, Dante follows the saints up the ladder; in a twinkling, he discovers himself in the House of Gemini, the sign of the Zodiac under which he was born. From that height Dante pauses to turn his gaze downward, and he smiles to see how small and in-significant the earth appears; he thinks how vain are the earthly goals men strive for and how much wiser are the persons who strive for spiri-tual goals. Next he observes and admires the seven planets beneath him, marveling at their circling and the great distances that separate them. Then after one more glance at "that little threshing floor that makes men fierce," he turns his eyes to the eyes of Beatrice.

Commentary

The second speaker to address Dante from among the lights on the golden ladder is, appropriately, St. Benedict, founder of the first great order of monks in western Europe. Early in the sixth century he founded the famous monastery on Monte Cassino in what had been a pagan temple, and he set down rigid rules for the monks of his order. His realization of the neglect and the abuse of those rules among his living followers provokes his bitter diatribe. This attack on the monastic orders, much in the spirit of that pronounced by Peter Damian in the previous canto, is also reminiscent of the denunciations of the Domini-cans by St. Thomas (*Par.* 11) and the Franciscans by St. Bonaventura (*Par.* 12).

The speed of Dante's ascent to the next region is described as quicker than one would pull his finger out of a fire. His arrival in the eighth sphere is described with his customary attention to astronomical details. He is in the House of Gemini, which is a significant choice not only because it was the sign of his birth date but also because it was under the influence of Gemini that he derived his love of learning. For this, he expresses his gratitude.

At this transitional point in his journey, the poet looks back to sur-vey the territory he has passed through. From his lofty vantage point, he sees the earth as a miniscule dot in the universe, and he reflects on the vanity of all the worldly hopes men set their hearts upon. Such a view of earth and the concomitant scornful reflections belong to a literary tradition stemming from Cicero's *Dream of Scipio* and Boethius' *On the Consolation of Philosophy* and recurring in Chaucer's *House of Fame* and *Troilus and Criseyde,* as well as in the epics of Ariosto and Tasso and a good many other poets long before the development of aviation or the space flights of the astronauts.

In his sweeping survey of the circling spheres, Dante indicates the various planets by indirect references rather than by their familiar

names for the benefit of his educated audience. Thus the moon is "Latona's daughter" and Mercury and Venus are designated as the children
of Maia and Dione, respectively. Jupiter stands between, and is tem-
pered by, the heat from his son Mars and the chill of his father Saturn.

CANTO 23

Summary

As Beatrice stands looking upward expectantly, Dante follows her
example and is soon rewarded with a scene of intense splendor. Beatrice, her countenance aflame, announces the approach of Christ in
triumph, and Dante sees many lights surrounding one great light, a
scene resembling the moon surrounded by the stars. This great light,
however, is of such brilliance that the poet is forced to lower his eyes.
Beatrice tells him to open his eyes and look at her, for now he has
gained the power to behold her smiling. The beauty of that smile is such
that it induces in him a state of ecstasy that he cannot adequately describe.

After Dante's brief glance at her, Beatrice bids him turn his view
once again to the heavenly scene. The light of Christ is soaring far
above, and now he perceives the Rose "in whom God's word was made
flesh" (Mary) and the lilies "whose fragrance led men to the good path-
way" (the apostles). A flaming light, shaped like a diadem and spinning
like a wheel (Gabriel), descends and circles the Rose, surrounding it
with such sweet music that it would make earth's finest harmonies
sound like a thunderclap. As the circling diadem of light hymns in
Mary's honor, all the company of spirits sound her name.

Mary, following the course of her Son, rises toward the Empyrean,
which is so high above where Dante stands that his sight cannot follow
her. As she rises, the surrounding lights, reaching upward to express
their affection, become pointed flames, as they sing *Regina coeli.*

What a rich reward, the poet exclaims, is reserved for those devout
apostles who lived their earthly lives in righteousness!

Commentary

In this new region of heaven, Dante looks upward and is greeted
with a special vision, the triumph of Christ and Mary, who have descended from the Empyrean to greet the soul as it rises toward the

highest heaven. The fact that Dante cannot endure the brilliance of the divine Christ is in accordance with Church teaching. The triumph of Mary, which Dante is able to view after Christ's ascent, is spectacularly accompanied by Gabriel's circling light and the sweet music of the choiring saints.

The many lights surrounding Christ and Mary in this scene represent a special band among the blessed, the apostles and the prophets.

> Here triumphs, under the great Son
> Of God and Mary, in his victory,
> With both the ancient council and the new,
> He who holds the keys to so great glory.

The ancient council refers to the prophets of the Old Testament; the new council is composed of the apostles. "He who holds the keys" is St. Peter. The glorious reward for those spirits who "wept in exile in Babylon" (suffered on earth) is hailed by the poet.

To impress the reader with the splendor of this scene, Dante has introduced an abundance of delightful figures that enrich the passage.

CANTO 24

Summary

Beatrice, addressing the band of spirits there as those invited to the supper of the Lamb of God, begs that they will favor her companion with some crumbs from their table. In response, they form themselves into spheres that turn in varied motion, some swift, some slow. Then one bright light detaches itself from its group and offers to satisfy her request. She recognizes the spirit as that great man "to whom the Savior bequeathed the keys" and requests him to test Dante on his conception of faith.

Like a doctoral candidate preparing for an oral examination, Dante braces his mind. To the initial question, "What is faith?" he answers that the essence of it is summed up in Paul's words: " . . . the substance of things hoped for, the evidence of things not seen" (Heb. 11). His examiner then asks how he understands "substance" and "evidence" in that definition. In his response Dante states that those subjects of mystery that are hidden from those on earth are revealed in heaven and their existence in heaven constitutes the substance of belief for men;

in dealing with theological questions — the mysteries — one is obliged to reason from beliefs, in syllogistic manner. Thus do beliefs serve as our evidence.

The examiner declares his satisfaction with the answer, then asks Dante how he came to this understanding. He answers that it came to him through the Holy Scriptures concerned with miracles. The next question is: "How do you know that you can believe the accounts of the miracles?" The answer is that the success of Christianity in converting the world, had it come about without miracles, would have been the greatest of miracles.

Finally Dante pronounces the basis of his credo: "I believe in one God, sole and eternal, who, unmoved, moves all heaven with love and desire. . . . I believe in the Trinity. . . ." The saint, well pleased with all of Dante's responses, expresses his joy by circling around the candidate three times.

Commentary

In the eighth heaven Dante is subjected to a series of examinations in preparation for his ascent to the two higher heavens. The examinations are concerned with his understanding of the three Christian virtues, faith, hope, and love; the examiners are to be the three favorite apostles, Peter, James, and John. The present canto records the examination on faith conducted by St. Peter. Peter is an appropriate figure to speak on the subject of faith because of his part in the incident of walking on the water and his being the first to enter the tomb of Christ on Easter morning.

The procedure for the examination is reminiscent of that of a candidate for the doctorate in philosophy. The answers of the candidate, being derived from the Scriptures or from Augustine and Aquinas and wholly orthodox, are received by St. Peter not only with approbation but with delight. The tone of this passage, that of sober dialectic discourse, is in striking and deliberate contrast with the rapturous, poetic style of the preceding canto.

CANTO 25

Summary

In the opening lines Dante states that if the fame of his poem opens the way for him to return to Florence, he will enter proudly to receive the poet's crown in the Baptistry because he first entered into the Christian faith there, the faith that has now been hailed by Peter.

A new light now approaches which Beatrice recognizes as the apostle whose shrine in Galicia attracts so many pilgrims (St. James). She asks the saint to discourse on hope, since he was the apostle distinguished for that virtue. The saint reminds them that Dante's journey to heaven before his death is for the purpose of confirming his hope of heavenly reward and that of others still alive. He then asks Dante, "What is hope?"

Before Dante can reply, Beatrice speaks, declaring that there is no man living more confirmed in hope than Dante, the proof of which is his dispensation to journey to Paradise while still alive. She then defers to Dante to discuss matters concerning hope which will not give occasion for boasting on his part.

Dante defines hope as the certain expectation of future glory which is attained through divine grace and precedent merit. How did he learn of this? Through many inspiring guides, he says, first through David in the Psalms and also from the Epistle of James. What does hope promise? Both the Old and New Testaments promise hope for all those that God wills to dwell with Him. Isaiah promises that each shall be clad in a double garment "in his own promised land" (heaven); and John (James' brother) expresses that same hope in Revelations. At the conclusion of the interrogation there is heard singing from above, *Sperent in te* ("They hope in Thee").

A third shining light now descends from a sphere of lights and joins the two apostles with whom the poet has conversed, and the three lights dance joyfully together. Beatrice introduces the third as ". . . he that lay on the breast of [Christ] our Pelican" and received the great charge from the cross (St. John). Dante, following Beatrice's gaze, stares at the new light until he is blinded. The spirit chides Dante for staring at him so intently as if he expected to see his bodily form, for it lies buried in the earth.

Abruptly all is hushed, and Dante turns to Beatrice only to discover that he cannot see her though she is close beside him.

Commentary

The canto dedicated to hope opens with lines suggesting what Dante may do if his poetry wins him reinstatement as a citizen of his native Florence, pathetic evidence that such was a fond hope that he cherished until his last years.

The apostle chosen to conduct the examination on hope is St. James. Typically, he is not named in the text but is identified through reference to his famous shrine in Galicia, Spain, at Campostella. As James opens the questioning in the customary manner, Beatrice intercedes to spare Dante an occasion for self-praise, assuring the saint that Dante is as sound in hope as any living man, a fact confirmed by his journey to heaven before his natural death. This last is stated in allusive language: ". . . therefore it is granted that he come from Egypt (earth) to Jerusalem (heaven) before his warfare is finished."

From the definition that Dante offers of hope, it is clear that he is treating the specific concept of a theological virtue, not the broader general concept of the term. Hope is the certain expectation of *heavenly reward.* It depends on two requirements, heavenly grace and past performance of good deeds. The sources of this knowledge, he says, are many, of which he cites two: a passage in the Psalms and one in the Epistle of James. The passage from James that he has in mind is in Chapter 1, verse 12. This, however, involves a confusion of Jameses, for in Dante's day James of the Epistle and the apostle James were thought to be the same person.

In answer to the question concerning the promise of hope, Dante cites a passage from Isaiah to the effect that the blessed one shall wear a double garment in his own country. The standard interpretation of the passage is that the body and soul would be joined in heaven. A second biblical reference is to the promise of white robes in St. John's Revelations. Again Dante is mistaken in believing that John, the brother of James, and John of Revelations are the same person.

The third apostle makes his appearance, John, "the beloved disciple." Beatrice introduces him as "he who rested on the breast of our Pelican. . . ." The pelican was a familiar symbol for Christ. The great charge which John received from the cross was to care for Mary.

John assures Dante that he does not have his bodily form here, that only two humans have their bodily forms in heaven, Christ and Mary, and that John must wait like all other souls until the Resurrection for the reunion of body and soul. The point here is that there was a belief current that John had been transported to heaven while living.

The effulgence of John's light is such that Dante is struck blind by looking at it intently; this blindness will last throughout the remainder of his conversation with John.

CANTO 26

Summary

John assures the fearful Dante that his blindness is not permanent and that Beatrice has the power to heal him. Dante is content, for it was through his eyes, through his seeing her, that she first brought the fire that kindles him. He declares that whatever good pleases heaven is all the direction that his love requires. The saint then asks who inspired him to so high a goal. This, Dante answers, came to him through philosophic argument and through authority, that is to say, through reason and revelation. Some of his understanding he owes to Aristotle, some to God's words to Moses, and some to John's writings in his gospel.

When asked to explain what has bound him so firmly to the love of God, Dante states that of the many forces inclining his heart to God, the foremost is the sacrifice of Christ through his death. Then, by way of a conclusion, he declares his love for all of God's creatures in proportion to the degree of blessedness God has bestowed on them.

Dante's pronouncements are greeted with lovely singing by the spirits and with "Holy, holy, holy!" from Beatrice. His sight is then restored, by means of Beatrice's brightness so that his vision is better than before. He first sees a new light, the fourth to greet him. The new spirit, whom Beatrice identifies as Adam, excites Dante's curiosity; but he waits for Adam to speak, knowing that he knows what is in Dante's mind. Adam's first revelation is that his exile from the Garden was not in punishment for eating the apple but for his disobedience. He then says that he spent 4,302 years in Limbo after his life on earth that lasted 930 years. To the question of what language he spoke in the Garden of Eden, he says it was lost even before the Tower of Babel episode. It is natural for men's languages to change because they are the inventions of human reason. Adam's final revelation is that the duration of his stay in the Garden was only six hours.

Commentary

The poet's first intimation of what love means to him lies in the remark concerning Beatrice, who first opened his eyes to "the fire that

88

kindles me still." He then avers that for him the object and center of love is the will of heaven, which is to say love for God. Questioned about the source of his assurance concerning love, he credits philosophy and revelation, first citing Aristotle—who discusses the attributes of the First Mover, *Metaphysics XI*—and then the Bible. In his biblical citations, he refers to passages in both the Old and the New Testaments, a practice he has observed consistently through all his discussions in the eighth sphere.

In asking Dante what has bound him so firmly in his love for God, John uses a striking, unconventional figure of speech: "With what teeth does this love bite thee?" The answer Dante gives is that Christ's sacrifice for mankind is the chief binding force for him. Then, as his final statement, he likens a gardener to the Creator and the leaves in the garden as the expression of His love for all His creatures.

The discourse with St. John on love being concluded, Dante's sight is restored stronger than before. He then is greeted by Adam, who answers many of the questions that men of Dante's age puzzled over: how much time did he spend in the Garden? How long was his life on earth? How long was he in Limbo before Christ released him? And what language did he speak? The figures Adams gives are as precise as one could wish. However the short period in the Garden before the banishment, six hours, may come as a surprise to modern readers. Adam's long life after the Fall is supported by a passage in Genesis. He was 930 years old when he died, and he spent 4,302 years in Limbo before Christ rescued him. It may be supposed that Dante understood Christ's age at the time of his descent into Hell as thirty-two, which would put the creation of Adam exactly 5,200 years before the birth of Christ.

When Adam says that the language he spoke was lost before the affair of the Tower of Babel brought about the confusion of tongues, this represents a change of opinion on Dante's part; in his *De Vulgari Eloquentia* he expressed the opinion that Adam spoke Hebrew. Evidently his later study of languages led him to realize that a language without a written literature could not continue long without change.

CANTO 27

Summary

As the heavenly host sings to the Father, Son, and Holy Ghost, the whole universe seems to smile and Dante experiences a moment of inebriate rapture. The four brightest lights stand shining before Dante, but now the light of St. Peter takes on an intense and fiery glow. The saint proceeds to deliver a scathing denunciation of the modern papacy for its degeneracy and corruption. Recent popes have turned his tomb into a sewer choked with blood and filth. The founding of the Church through the blood and sacrifices of the early popes (Linus, Sixtus, Urban, etc.) was not for gain of gold, nor was it intended that the keys of the office should be an emblem in battle against fellow Christians, as it is now. Let these recent popes (Cahorsines and Gascons) beware, for vengeance is not far off. Peter now admonishes Dante to speak out boldly against these vices when he returns to earth.

The scene in the Sphere of Fixed Stars closes with the ascent of all the apostles and prophets, resembling a sparkling snowstorm disappearing into the heavens. Dante takes one last look downward at the earth, discovering that his position has changed during his discourse here. He is now over Gibraltar, and the eastern half of the Mediterranean is in shadow because of the position of the sun. Turning his gaze back to Beatrice, he is entranced with the sight of her radiant countenance; and as he gazes, they are transported to "the swiftest of the heavens."

Beatrice informs Dante that the sphere they have reached, the Primum Mobile or Crystalline Sphere, is the base from which all of the lower spheres receive the impetus for their motion and that this sphere is powered by the force of God's love. Now, she says, it should be clear to Dante how time has its roots in this sphere and its leaves in the other spheres. She then complains that covetousness has taken control over mankind. It is not that men are vicious by nature, for in childhood they display innocence and faith; but as they grow older, they turn to evil ways and, especially now, no one in the world governs well. There is a promise, however, that the future will bring a light from heaven that will guide men on an altered course.

Commentary

St. Peter speaks again but in a different role from that of an examiner on faith. Here he speaks as the founder of the papacy, voicing his disgust over the conduct of the recent popes. He singles out the pope reigning at the time Dante was writing *Paradiso*, Pope John XXII, and John's immediate predecessor, Clement V, both of whom Dante attacked in earlier passages. The Gascon pope, Clement V, was responsible for transferring the papal seat from Rome to Avignon *(Par. 17)*. The native of Cahors, John XXII, got rich through his practice of excommunicating kings and nobles who would pay generously for their reinstatement.

As the author looks down on the little globe of earth, he indicates with utmost precision his position with reference to the earth, the sun, and the zodiac, though his references are in oblique language. He is still in the sign of Gemini, and he can see where Ulysses ventured on his last voyage. The sun is ahead of him by about 40°, so that a part of the earth's surface within his view is shaded from the sun, that is, the Phoenician coast, where Europa started her journey mounted on the bull.

The physical nature of the ninth heaven is presented in vague terms. It is called crystalline because it is colorless as well as transparent. Dante must have thought of it as extending into virtually limitless space, for there is nothing beyond it save that it is embraced by the Empyrean, which is the Mind of God. Its influence on the other spheres as their driving force is a familiar concept that has been mentioned in several earlier passages.

Time is compared to a plant: its roots in the Primum Mobile are not visible to man, but the leaves of the plant are the planets, by which our time is measured.

Beatrice inveighs against the present decay of morals, which she attributes to the dominance of covetousness. Dante's embittered view of the state of the world, here expressed in the words of Beatrice, is countered, as it invariably has been throughout the *Comedy*, by a prophecy of a better time to come under the rule of a heaven-sent leader. God will not allow such viciousness to endure. In this instance the promised time for the coming of the brave new world is rather more remote than usual. The date when January would be advanced to spring would be far removed from Dante's age. According to the Julian calendar then in use, the year was computed a small fraction of a day longer than the true sidereal year, with the result that January started a little later in the season every year. To wait until January would be in the spring season would have required almost ninety centuries.

CANTO 28

Summary

Dante is given a sight that reveals God in relation to the orders of angels, but his first awareness of the vision comes to him through the reflected light in the eyes of Beatrice. When he discovers the extraordinary light in her eyes, he turns to see a tiny dot of intense brightness that is surrounded by nine concentric circles of light. The brightness of the circles is in proportion to their closeness to the central dot of light; similarly, the closer the circles are to the center, the more swiftly they move. Dante is puzzled by this pattern, since it is contrary to the condition and movement of the planetary spheres. The explanation given by his guide is that these spheres derive their light and energy from God, who is the central light of the system, and their benefits are in ratio to their proximity. God is beyond the planetary spheres; consequently, the outer ones move at greater speeds.

The circles of light are composed of showers of sparks. Beatrice, responding to Dante's unspoken question, begins to identify the orders of angels in the circling spheres. Starting with the innermost, the swiftest and brightest, and progressing outward, she names the first triad as the Seraphim, the Cherubim, and the Thrones. These are especially blessed by their intimate sight of the Creator and are graced with superior powers of intelligence. In the second triad are the Dominations, the Virtues, and the Powers, creating harmonious descants with their Hosannas. The last triad is composed of the Principalities, the Archangels, and the Angels. All of these angelic orders gaze upward; at the same time, their influences are impelled downward toward their appropriate spheres in the physical universe.

Citing the principal authors who have treated the subject of angelic orders, Beatrice mentions first Dionysius and then Pope Gregory I. The latter's theories differed somewhat with the former but, she declares, Dionysius was correct.

Commentary

The scene, or vision, that is presented to Dante here reveals the relation of the Godhead to the angels. The fact that this image is first revealed as a reflection in Beatrice's eyes is meant to suggest that it is a truth transmitted through revelation, which Beatrice symbolizes.

The angels, classified in nine separate orders, are described as spheres, ranged according to their degrees of holiness and, consequently, of influence. Each of them acts on one of the nine heavenly spheres and is identified as the "Intelligence" controlling that sphere. The highest order in rank, the Seraphim (Hebrew plural of seraph), dominate the Primum Mobile. The Cherubim control the Fixed Stars; the Thrones control Saturn, and so on down in order.

92

The number of sparks in the spheres is compared to the progressive doubling of the numbers of squares on a chessboard. The reference is to an ancient Eastern legend: a king, wishing to reward the man who invented chess, asked what he wanted for a reward. The man said he would like a grain of wheat doubled for every square on the chessboard. The count proved to be astronomical.

The idea that angels should be classified and ranked according to their virtues and powers was universally taught in the Middle Ages and considerably later (See Milton, for example). It was in conformity with the general idea that every aspect of the scheme of creation was hierarchical, the basis for "the Great Chain of Being." The author who first announced the number and arrangement of the classes of angels was Dionysius the Areopagite, who was said to have received his information from St. Paul. Pope Gregory I, "the Great," proposed some modifications of Dionysius' plan, but as he was to learn when he reached heaven himself, he was mistaken.

CANTO 29

Summary

Beatrice pauses briefly, gazing toward the shining dot which is God. She then begins to resolve several questions regarding angels that she knows Dante would wish to have answered. God, with whom there is no *where* and no *when*, created the angels as a reflection of his splendor. Their creation and the combining of form and matter came about in a single moment. "Pure form (or act)," the summit of creation, is the angels; "pure matter (or potency)" signifies matter without form; the combining of form and matter (act and potency) produced the heavenly bodies. St. Jerome was mistaken in his conjecture that the angels existed long before the universe of spirit and matter.

Not long after the creation of the angels, Beatrice reports, a band of rebel angels was cast out of heaven, creating a great disturbance on earth. The rest of the angels have remained in heaven ever circling and reflecting the Divine Presence. The faculties ascribed to the angels by various mortals are confused, some claiming that they possess understanding, memory, and will. Beatrice explains that they have no use for memory since they are perpetually occupied in one activity.

Beatrice now comments on some of the foibles and abuses practiced by theologians and preachers. The kind of idle speculation just spoken of would be considered relatively harmless were it not practiced at the expense of serious teaching and preaching of the Gospel. Preachers who devote their sermons to fantastic tales and to "getting a laugh" are culpable and are courting Satan.

To give some impression of the vast number of angels in those spheres, Beatrice refers to a passage in the Book of Daniel, which is not specific in its thousands. The prime light from the Godhead is sent back by the angels in different fashion, reflecting in diverse colors the variations in the sweetness of love as from a multitude of mirrors.

Commentary

The "children of Latona" cited in the opening passage of the canto are Apollo and Diana, the sun and the moon. This astronomical figure speaks of a brief moment at the vernal equinox when the sun and moon are exactly opposite, one rising and one setting. The sun is in the sign of Aries and the moon is in the sign of Libra. This situation lasts only a fleeting moment.

Through much of this canto, Beatrice continues her instruction concerning the nature of angels, a subject that fascinated medieval audiences. She settles unequivocally the question of whether the angels were created before, or at the same time, that form and matter were united. She mentions, though only briefly, the revolt of the angels, reminding Dante of the condition in which he saw Satan in the pit of Inferno.

Speaking of some of the fanciful speculations engaged in concerning angels, Beatrice takes the occasion to condemn certain preachers who devote their sermons to ingenious imaginings about such matters as whether or not angels have memory or whether the entire earth was darkened at the time of the Crucifixion. Meanwhile they neglect preaching the Gospel to their congregations. Her censure of such errant preachers includes a disparaging association between them and pigs. Because a pig was associated with St. Anthony, swine belonging to monks were treated as sacred and were permitted to feed anywhere. The monks, in gratitude, gave out pardons freely, which pardons, Beatrice maintains, are invalid and will give their recipients a false sense of security.

CANTO 30

Summary

The gradual fading and final disappearance of the lights in the angelic orders is compared to the dimming of stars, first near the horizon, and then over the whole sky just before sunrise.

With the vision gone, Dante turns to Beatrice again. If all that he has previously said of her beauty were added together, it could not express what beauty he now sees in her; he confesses himself hopelessly defeated in the attempt. Since he first saw her on earth, her beauty has been the constant theme of his verse, but henceforth he must forego that theme as beyond his powers.

Beatrice announces that they have risen to the region of pure light, the heaven of heavens, where Dante will see both angels and saints assembled. By special dispensation he will be permitted to see the saints clothed in their corporeal forms as they will appear at the Resurrection.

A bright light blinds the poet but only for a moment, and when he regains his sight, it has been strengthened so that he can endure any brightness. He now sees a great river of light flowing between two flowery banks. Sparks rise out of the river, fly to the flowers, and then— as if intoxicated—return to the river. At Beatrice's bidding, Dante "drinks" from the river by touching his eyes to it, whereupon the river is transformed into a sea, and the sparks and flowers assume a new pattern. The form is that of a great rose whose center is a wonderful light, whose petals are in more than a thousand tiers, and whose expanse would more than girdle the sun. Beatrice calls attention to the immense throng of spirits and to the few unfilled places in the tiers. She then directs his attention to one empty seat marked with a crown which is reserved for the Emperor Henry VII, who, she says, will come to free Italy, though his attempt is doomed to failure. The pope who will contribute to that failure by his underhanded opposition will not rule long and will be punished in Inferno in the company of Simon Magus and Boniface VIII.

Commentary

Here again a canto opens with an elaborate astronomical image describing the dimming of the stars just before dawn. A man located

6,000 miles west of where the sun is shining at noon would be more than 90 degrees from the sun and thus in darkness. Ninety degrees of the earth's circumference, according to Dante's information, would be 5,100 miles. The observer would be within the shadow of the earth but near sunrise. However, there is a time before the sunlight reaches the man when it touches the sky on the eastern horizon because the shadow of the earth is conical. This complex image serves to describe the fading of the angelic lights as the pilgrims soar to the Empyrean.

One of the phenomenal achievements in *Paradiso* is the glorification of Beatrice's ever increasing beauty, which reaches its climax in this magnificent passage. It is interesting that in this moment Dante remembers his first sight of Beatrice in his childhood. It is also characteristic that she quickly resumes her role as guide and teacher.

The sense of sight has played a major role throughout the poem. Here it is given very special prominence. Dante is blinded so that he may attain a new faculty of vision. The river of light is symbolic of divine grace; the sparks from the river are angels; and the flowers to which they are ministering are the souls of the blessed. Dante is granted an entire new vision of heaven through dipping his eyelids in the stream of light. The heart of the Rose is the omnipotent light of God, and surrounding it are rows on rows of the angels and the saints. Of the thousands upon thousands of "seats" in the Rose, most are filled, signifying that Dante did not expect the world to last much longer. In the *Convivio* (II, xv) he had said, "We are already in the last age of the world."

Emperor Henry VII is awarded a singular tribute in this scene. This and earlier references to Henry are necessarily treated as prophecies because of the supposed date of Dante's journey. Henry did not come to the throne until 1308. It should be recalled that Dante had pinned his hopes of the restoration of imperial authority in Italy on Henry. Even though Henry died before he could accomplish his mission, Dante honors him with a high station in Paradise in contrast with the fate assigned to the pope who opposed Henry, Clement V ("prefect of the divine forum"). Beatrice reminds Dante that a place is reserved for that pope in Malebolgia along with Simon Magus and Clement's predecessor, Boniface VIII ("him of Anagni"). Thus the cause of the empire against the papacy is recognized again in heaven.

The reminder of a passage far, far back among the scenes of *Inferno*, together with the reference in the preceding canto to Satan in *Inferno*, is a remarkably effective means of calling to our minds the long journey we have taken and consequently helping to unify the total pattern of this extremely complex poem.

CANTO 31

Summary

The souls of the redeemed, clad in white raiment, fill the great Rose. Angels, like a swarm of bees, fly about, dipping down into the heart of the Rose and soaring up to touch its petals. Their faces are of living flame, their wings of gold, their clothing whiter than the purest snow. All eyes are turned toward a star that gleams with a triple light. Dante, who has recently come from the corrupt world to the heavenly city, is filled with a wonderful joy; silently he views the faces of the blessed.

When he wishes to question Beatrice, he turns only to find that she is gone and in her place stands a saintly elder, who points to Beatrice in her seat among the blessed. Dante eloquently expresses his gratitude to her; and though they are separated by a great distance, she hears him and she turns and smiles. The new guide tells him to gaze on "this garden" in order to prepare his eyes for God's luminance. He tells Dante that he is St. Bernard, and he assures Dante that the Queen of Heaven will grant him grace. He then tells Dante to look up to the highest tier where sits the Queen, enthroned in brilliant light and surrounded by more than a thousand angels flying and singing joyfully. Her light is of a beauty that brings joy to the other saints. St. Bernard's expression in looking at her shines with such love that it inspires Dante with greater eagerness.

Commentary

The climactic effect that the poet is building toward depends on the same sensory characteristics that we have seen throughout *Paradiso*, light in moving patterns and music. In order to dramatize effects, he often resorts to reporting his emotional responses. One detail that adds to the psychological appeal in this scene is that saints and angels are no longer spots of light but appear in their individual incarnate forms.

Concrete visual images, conveyed through similes, contribute to the effectiveness of the scene. Dante's amazement at the spectacle of the Rose is compared to that of the Goths upon first entering Rome. (The reference to Helice is to the maiden transformed into the Great

Bear or Dipper, her son being the Little Bear. Saying that the barbarians
came from the region spanned by Helice and her son is Dante's way of
saying they came from the far north.) In another figure, the poet compares his concentrated gaze with that of a pilgrim from Croatia who has
come to see the Veronica in Rome and cannot take his eyes away as
long as the relic is being shown.

The most dramatic feature of the narrative in this canto is that there
is a transfer of guides. Beatrice leaves her pupil to take her place in the
Rose, and St. Bernard replaces her as final instructor and intermediary.
The departure of Beatrice is without warning and without farewells, a
circumstance reminiscent of the departure of Virgil in the Earthly
Paradise. Beatrice has a place of high honor in the upper third row of
the Rose.

In her role as Dante's guide Beatrice represents Revelation, the
kind of intelligence necessary for direction through Paradise, as distinct
from Reason, the intelligence of Virgil. Now that Dante has been
brought to the heaven of heavens with the aid of Reason and Revelation,
a new mentor is assigned before his vision of the Divine Presence. This
guide, St. Bernard, represents Intuition. He is chosen for this role because he is peculiarly qualified to intercede with Mary, who is the final
intercessor to the Trinity. Bernard of Clairvaux, a twelfth-century
French monk, was especially known for his devotion to the Virgin. In
fact, it was he, probably more than any other man, who was responsible
for the great upsurge in the veneration of Mary which marked the later
Middle Ages. The role of Mary in Christianity during this period, so
beautifully demonstrated through the dedication of the great Gothic
cathedrals (Notre Dame, for example), is nowhere more clearly revealed
in literature than in the *Divine Comedy*. This canto gives us a dramatic
sight of her in all her glory on the highest tier of the great Rose.

CANTO 32

Summary

St. Bernard explains the arrangement of the spirits within the celestial assembly and identifies certain saints who occupy places of honor.
On the second tier from the top and seated just at the feet of Mary is
Eve. On the third tier is Rachel and beside her is Beatrice. Then in
descending tiers are Sarah, Rebecca, Judith, and Ruth. These and many
more Old Testament women in a vertical row form a dividing line between those who believed in Christ though He was yet unborn and

98

those who believed after His coming. Among the former group, the seats are all occupied, but amid the latter there are places still unfilled.

Directly opposite Mary and the line of Hebrew women is St. John the Baptist and a row of male saints, headed by St. Francis, St. Benedict, and St. Augustine. Thus we see that the basic pattern separates the men from the women, though the plan is not entirely consistent in this respect.

The upper sections of the Rose are for adults; the lower sections are taken by infants who died before they attained the age of moral responsibility. Their salvation is won for them through the faith of others. Bernard points out that God has decreed various degrees of blessedness among the infants, citing the marked differences between Jacob and Esau although they were twins. He explains that in addition to the faith of the child's parents, a ceremonial act is called for. In the case of ancient Hebrew children, it was circumcision; in the case of Christians, baptism.

At St. Bernard's bidding, Dante again lifts his eyes toward Mary, whose brightness can prepare him for the refulgence of Christ. The joy expressed on the faces of the angels surrounding her is beyond anything he has yet seen. Gabriel spreads his great wings before her, and to the hymn *Ave Maria, gratia plena,* the entire court of heaven sings responses.

Dante asks who the angel is that is gazing at the Queen with such rapture and is told that he is the one who brought Mary the news that she would bear the Christ-child. Then his instructor identifies other figures closest to Mary, Adam on one side, Peter on the other; beside Peter, John the Apostle, and beside Adam, Moses. Opposite St. Peter is St. Anne, and opposite Adam sits St. Lucy.

St. Bernard, reminding Dante that his time in Paradise is limited, advises him that to penetrate the Divine Image he must obtain grace from Christ's mother.

Commentary

The blessed who are singled out for mention in the heavenly court are those we should expect in the conception of a medieval Christian. If anything surprises the reader, it is the restraint exercised by the author, for there must have been a strong temptation to mention many more holy names. Many readers must wonder why their favorite saint was not cited, but a longer list would certainly have become tedious. Most of the honored figures are simply mentioned by name; a few are introduced through characterizing phrases. Eve is indicated as she who opened the wound that Mary healed, the wound caused by eating the apple. She not only caused the wound but deepened it by feeding the apple to Adam. Ruth is mentioned simply as the great-grandmother of the singer (David) who sang *Miserere mei* (Psalms 51). "The great John" who dwelt in the wilderness and spent two years in Limbo is St. John the Baptist. He died two years before the Harrowing of Hell.

When Dante is directed to look at the face that bears the greatest resemblance to Christ's, that face is Mary's. The angel who came down to greet Mary, singing *Ave Maria, gratia plena* is, of course, Gabriel. Of Mary's immediate companions, the one whose "rash tasting" caused mankind such bitterness is Adam. The "Father of Holy Church" to whom Christ entrusted the keys to this glorious flower (the heavenly Rose) is St. Peter.

The presence of infants in heaven is based on accepted doctrine. For their admission what is necessary is the faith of their parents plus the performance of a ceremonial act, baptism for Christians or circumcision for pre-Christians. The question of whether all children enjoy equal blessedness or whether there are degrees of blessedness bestowed by God is settled by Dante in favor of the latter concept. On this point he differs from St. Thomas. He finds support for his position in the story of Jacob and Esau, who fought in their mother's womb and who were born with radically different physical and temperamental characteristics.

CANTO 33

Summary

The final canto opens with a prayer to the Virgin on Dante's behalf spoken by St. Bernard. He commences with an invocation which recites the magnificent attributes of the mother of Christ, to whom men pray for blessings from heaven because of her motherly tenderness toward mankind and her influential voice before the Almighty. He then beseeches grace for Dante that he may be granted the vision of God and that he may have the skill to report his vision for future generations.

The Virgin's eyes reveal how she is gratified by devout prayers; she lifts her gaze toward the Eternal Light, at which sign Bernard indicates to Dante that his wish has been granted, and Dante looks up into the Light.

The glorious vision that comes to the poet is almost wholly lost to his memory. His experience was like that of a dreamer who on waking cannot recall the substance of his dream but still feels the emotion it stirred in him. He invokes the Almighty to grant him power to recall at least a spark of the glory of it so that he will be able to transmit it to his fellow men.

He tells us that he gazed steadily into the Light until his sight was united with the Infinite Good, and within that Light he saw bound together all of the various pages of the volume of the universe. There he perceived all the world's substance joined in such a way that it appeared a simple unity. So much was comprehended in that vision that what he forgot after its passing exceeded all that was forgotten of the enterprise of the Argonauts in twenty-five centuries. But this he knows, that he saw there the Good which is the object of the Will.

For that small part of the vision which he holds in remembrance, his language is no more adequate than the speech of a suckling babe. The fullness of that experience was made possible because his faculties were transfigured. Within that single Light he saw three circles of different colors mutually reflecting one another. Finally, within one circle he saw the human image, a sight which fascinates and at the same time perplexes him deeply. Then there came a flash of revelation; his desires and will were brought into perfect conformity, incited by the power of Love, "the Love that moves the sun and the other stars."

Commentary

Bernard's prayer to Mary, spoken on Dante's behalf, compresses into thirty-nine lines the full spirit of Mariolatry which plays so great a role in the Christianity of the age. A prayer to Mary was believed to win a sympathetic ear and hence an influential advocate with Christ. The sweetness and gentleness, the mother-child relationship of Mary to mankind, was ultimately related to the new attitude toward women that so greatly transformed Western culture in the later Middle Ages.

As the final and climactic scene of the *Comedy*, Dante wishes to report his mystic experience, coming into the presence of God, yet he knows that he dare not present the episode in terms wholly explicit. He ascribes the vagueness of his remembrance to the overwhelming power of the moment in which his human faculties were miraculously transfigured. If he cannot relate *in toto* the physical aspects of the revelation, he can still retain the emotional impact that it made on him. He knows that in the moment of revelation he saw the complex universe as a unified whole and that his will was merged with the World-Will. This is in conformity with a familiar definition of mysticism: "to recognize unity in diversity and permanence in change."

What he can recapture of the vision is the image of the Trinity, for within that single Light were visible three circles, coexistent, of different colors; and within one of the circles, wonderful to tell, the image of man. That circle, of course, represents the Son, who took on mortality; but it will not escape the reader that the image carries the implication that there is some spark of divinity in man himself.

When Milton announces in *Paradise Lost* that he proposes to "assert Eternal Providence," he is expressing Dante's precise intention, for this scene in Paradise is his way of expressing his belief in God. The rest of Milton's claimer helps further to describe the *Divine Comedy*.

> That to the highth of this great Argument
> I may assert Eternal Providence,
> And justify the ways of God to men.

SELECTED LIST OF CHARACTERS

The number in parentheses following the name refers to the canto in which the character appears or is cited.

Albert I of Austria (19). Emperor 1298-1308. Censured by Dante for his invasion of Bohemia. Cf. *Purg.* 6.

Albert of Cologne (10). "Albertus Magnus," famous theologian and teacher of Aquinas.

Alighiero (15). Dante's ancestor from whom the family name was derived.

Anchises (15, 19). Father of Aeneas.

Anne, St. (32). Mother of Mary.

Anselm (12). Archbishop of Canterbury, author and teacher.

Aquinas, St. Thomas (10-13). Theologian who wrote prolifically, who influenced Dante's religious thought more than anyone else, and whose authority over Catholic doctrine is still profound. A Dominican, he praises St. Francis, founder of the rival order of friars.

Ariadne (13). In Greek mythology, she was the daughter of Minos; with her sister Phaedra she helped Theseus kill the Minotaur and escape from Crete. After being deserted by Theseus, she was married to Dionysus. At her death she was transported to heaven as a constellation, the Corona Borealis.

Aristotle (24, 26). Ancient Greek philosopher whose work was widely studied and much admired during the later Middle Ages, especially through the influence of Thomas Aquinas. Cf. *Inf.* 4; *Purg.* 3.

Arius (13). Early Christian leader responsible for the Arian heresy which was condemned by the Council of Nicaea.

Augustine, St. (10, 32). One of the most powerful early Church fathers, author of *Confessions* and *Civitas Dei*. He became Bishop of Hippo in North Africa.

Beatrice Portinari. A Florentine lady whom Dante knew and loved in his youth. She inspired his *Vita Nuova* and became his spiritual guide on his journey through Paradise.

Bede (10). Anglo-Saxon monk who wrote the *Ecclesiastical History of the English Nation.*

Benedict, St. (22, 32). Founder of the first monastic order in western Europe, the Benedictines. Their first monastery was established at Monte Cassino.

Bernard, St. (31-33). Religious leader in France in the twelfth century. He was a strong advocate of the Second Crusade. He did much to stimulate the rise of Mariolatry.

Boethius (10). A prominent sixth-century Roman statesman who was unjustly condemned to prison and death. In prison he wrote *On the Consolation of Philosophy.*

Bonaventura, St. (12). A prominent Franciscan. In the Sphere of the Sun he delivers a eulogy on St. Dominic.

Boniface VIII (9, 12, 27, 30). The reigning pope in 1300. Through his influence Dante and his party were exiled. He figures throughout the *Comedy* as the archenemy of the religious and political well-being of Europe. Cf. *Inf.* 15, 19, 27; *Purg.* 20.

Buondelmonti (16). A member of this family was murdered for jilting a girl of the Amidei family. The feud resulting developed into the Guelf and Ghibelline parties in Florence.

Cacciaguida (15-17). Dante's great-great-grandfather, who was killed in the second crusade. He greets Dante in the Sphere of Mars and predicts the miseries in store for the poet as an exile.

Caesar, Caius Julius (6, 11). Brilliant general and head of the Roman state under the Republic. Cf. *Inf.* 1, 4, 28; *Purg.* 18.

Caesar, Octavianus (6). The great-nephew of Julius Caesar. He was the first emperor of Rome, was given the title of Augustus.

Caesar, Tiberius (6). Successor of Augustus, emperor at the time of the Crucifixion.

Can Grande della Scala (Cf. Scala).

Charlemagne (6, 18). King of France who became the first emperor of the Holy Roman Empire, receiving the crown from Pope Leo III in 800.

Charles I of Anjou (8). He seized the crown of Naples and Sicily in 1265 with the support of the pope, defeating Manfred, leader of the Ghibelline faction. Cf. *Purg.* 7, 11, 20.

Charles II of Naples (6, 19). Son of Charles I of Anjou and the father of Charles Martel.

Charles Martel (8-9). Son of Charles II of Naples. He inherited the title of King of Hungary. He had visited Florence in 1294, and on meeting Dante in the Third Heaven he greets him as a friend.

Chrysostom, St. (12). Patriarch of Constantinople in the fourth century. He was sent into exile for his public rebuke of the Empress Theodosia for her wanton conduct.

Clement V, Pope (17, 27, 30). It was during his papacy (1305-14) that the Papal See was transferred to Avignon under pressure from Philip IV of France. Dante despised him for this action.

Clymene (17). Maiden loved by Apollo; the mother of Phaëthon.

Conrad III, Emperor (15). One of the leaders of the second crusade, by whom Cacciaguida, Dante's ancestor, was knighted.

Constance, Empress (3). Lady taken out of her convent to marry the Emperor Henry VI. She was the mother of Frederick II.

Constantine, Emperor (6, 20). Roman emperor who was the first Christian emperor and who established a second capital at Byzantium, renaming it Constantinople.

Creusa (9). First wife of Aeneas. She was lost during the flight of the family from burning Troy.

Cunizza (9). A lady of Treviso, north of Venice, sister of the notorious Ezzelino da Romano. Given to passionate amours in her early life, she turned to charity in her later years.

Damian, Peter (Cf. **Peter Damian**).

Demophoon (9). Greek warrior for whom Phillis committed suicide, imagining that he had deserted her.

Dido (9). Queen of Carthage, widow of Sycheus; she fell in love with her guest Aeneas. She killed herself when he sailed for Italy at the command of the gods. Cf. *Inf.* 6.

Dionysius the Areopagite (10, 28). A Greek who was converted to Christianity by St. Paul. He was regarded as an authority on the hierarchy of angels.

Dominic, St. (11-12). As founder of the Dominican order of friars, he was one of the most effective religious leaders of the Middle Ages.

Donati, Piccarda (Cf. **Piccarda Donati**).

Donatus (12). A church scholar of the fourth century, an authority on grammar.

Europa (28). Daughter of the King of Phoenicia; she was abducted by Jupiter in the form of a bull and carried to Crete.

Folco (Foulquet) (9). A troubadour who, after a life devoted to worldly pleasures, turned to the religious life and became Abbot of Torronet.

Francis, St. (11, 13, 22, 32). Founder of the order of Franciscan friars at the beginning of the thirteenth century. A Christlike figure who is one of the most revered saints of the Church.

Frederick II, Emperor (3). A sovereign whom Dante admired. He ruled the empire from Italy in the first half of the thirteenth century. Barbarossa was his grandfather, Constance his mother, and Manfred his bastard son.

Frederick II, King of Sicily (19). A descendant of the royal house of Aragon, rivals of the house of Anjou in Sicily, he ruled the kingdom from 1296 to 1337.

Gabriel (4, 9, 14, 23, 32). The archangel chiefly remembered as the angel of the Annunciation.

Glaucus (1). A fisherman who, after eating a certain plant, was transformed into a sea god, thus "transhumanized."

Godfrey of Bouillon (18). Commander-in-chief of the First Crusade. He liberated Jerusalem in five weeks.

Gratian (10). Twelfth-century Church scholar who was credited with bringing canon law and civil law into conformity.

Gregory I, Pope (Gregory the Great) (28). His papacy, 590-604. He sent missionaries to the Anglo-Saxons under St. Augustine of Canterbury. He was responsible for the adoption of the Gregorian chant as the official form of church music.

Hannibal (6). Great Carthaginian general who dealt the Romans many severe defeats but was finally defeated by Scipio.

Henry VII, Emperor (17, 30). The emperor (1308-1313) on whom Dante pinned his hopes of re-establishing imperial rule in Italy in opposition to papal secular control.

Hippolytus (17). Son of Theseus who was unjustly accused by his step-mother, Phaedra, and banished with his father's curse.

Hugh of St. Victor (12). A twelfth-century theologian who became prior of St. Victor's in Paris.

Innocent III, Pope (11). The pope who first gave official sanction to the order of Franciscans.

Isidore of Seville, St. (10). An ecclesiastical scholar of the late sixth and early seventh centuries, who wrote an encyclopedia of science.

James the Apostle, St. (25). One of the apostles closest to Christ. There was a famous shrine to him in Campostella, Spain.

Jason (2). Greek legendary hero who led the expedition of the Argonauts in quest of the Golden Fleece. According to tradition he was the first sailor. Medea, who helped him gain the Golden Fleece, became his wife but was later abandoned by him.

Jephthah (5). A leader of Israel who vowed that if God would give him victory in battle he would sacrifice the first living thing that greeted him. It was his daughter who came out first.

Jerome, St. (29). One of the great Church fathers. His translation of the Bible into Latin, known as the Vulgate, was the official text for the Church.

Joachim of Flora (12). An abbot of Calabria whose influence among spiritual Franciscans was considerable.

John the Baptist, St. (4, 31-33). Elder cousin of Jesus who preached the coming of the Messiah. Patron saint of Florence, his figure was on their gold coin, the florin.

John the Apostle, St. (4, 24, 25, 26, 32). Brother of St. James the Apostle, John was called the "beloved disciple." Dante apparently believed that the author of the Gospel of John and John the Evangelist, the author of Revelations, was the same person.

John XXII, Pope (27). Born in Cahors, France, he succeeded Clement V to the papacy in 1316. It was during his reign that Dante was writing the latter part of *Paradiso*.

Justinian, Emperor (5-6). Ruling the tottering Roman empire from Constantinople in the sixth century, he repelled barbarian invaders. He is renowned for his codification of Roman law.

Lavinia (6). Second wife of Aeneas. Her father, Latinus, was an Italian king who formed an alliance with Aeneas.

Lawrence, St. (4). He was martyred by being roasted over a grill and is always so represented in religious art. During his ordeal he refused to reveal the hidden treasures of the Church.

Leda (27). Disguised as a swan, Jupiter made love to her. She gave birth to Helen and the twins, Castor and Pollux, the Gemini.

Lucy, St. (32). One of the "Three Blessed Ladies" (with Mary and Beatrice) responsible for Dante's journey. Cf. *Inf.* 2, *Purg.* 9.

Maccabaeus, Judas (18). A general who was greatly honored in Jewish history; he delivered his people from the tyranny of the Syrians in the second century B.C.

Marsyas (1). A satyr who challenged Apollo to a musical duel. He was defeated and as punishment he was bound to a tree and flayed.

Michael, St. (4). An archangel, often referred to as the warrior angel and depicted in armor.

Minos (13). A legendary king of Crete who, after his death, became a judge in Hades. Cf. *Inf.* 5.

Mucius (4). Caius Mucius Scaevola, without flinching, held his hand in the fire until it was consumed. This was his self-inflicted punishment for having failed to kill Lars Porsena.

Nathan the Prophet (12). He rebuked King David for having sent Uriah to his death because he lusted after Uriah's wife.

Nebuchadnezzar (4). King of Babylon whose dreams were interpreted by Daniel.

Nimrod (26). King of Babylon whose people attempted to build the tower of Babel. The result of that experiment was that people began speaking a diversity of languages.

Orosius (10). A Spanish priest of the fifth century who is famous for his *Compendious History of the World.* This was one of the books translated in King Alfred's Anglo-Saxon library.

Pallas (6). A youthful Trojan follower of Aeneas who was killed in battle by Turnus.

Parmenides (12). An ancient Greek philosopher whose work was criticized by Aristotle.

Paul, St. (18, 21, 24, 26, 28). An early convert to Christianity, he was the author of Acts and several of the Epistles of the New Testament. A fountainhead of Christian doctrine and the greatest early missionary.

Peter, St. (9, 18, 21, 22, 24, 27, 32). A leader among Christ's disciples, he was given the keys to heaven to admit or exclude souls. As first Bishop of Rome, he was the source of papal authority.

Peter Damian (21). A monk of the eleventh century who worked for monastic reform. From abbot he rose to cardinal and served as papal legate on important missions.

Peter Lombard (10). Having studied under Abelard and Hugh of St. Victor, he taught theology at the Universities of Bologna and Paris. He is most famous for his collection of the sayings of the Church fathers.

Peter Mangiadore (12). A twelfth-century scholar of St. Victor; author of commentaries on the Bible.

Peter of Spain (12). A Spanish priest who was elected Pope John XXI in 1276; he died the following year.

Phaedra (17). Second wife of Theseus, she fell in love with her stepson Hippolytus. When he rejected her advances, she falsely accused him and forced his banishment.

Philip IV ("the Fair") (19). King of France who ruled from 1285 to 1314. He quarreled with Pope Boniface VIII, and he persuaded Pope Clement V to transfer the papal seat from Rome to Avignon.

Piccarda Donati (3). Sister of Forese (Cf. *Purg.* 23) and Corso (Cf. *Purg.* 24, *Par.* 17). They were cousins of Dante's wife.

Pius I, Bishop of Rome (27). Second-century exemplar of the virtuous early popes.

Pompey (6). A member of the "First Triumvirate" with Julius Caesar and Crassus. His rivalry with Caesar later led to civil war, and he was defeated at Pharsalia.

Quintius (15). Lucius Quintius Cincinnatus, better known as Cincinnatus, Dictator of Rome in 458 B.C. He was regarded as an exemplar of the highest virtues of the early Romans.

Rabanus Maurus (12). Archbishop of Mayence in the eighth and ninth centuries; a poet and a biblical commentator.

Rachel (32). Second wife of Jacob; mother of Joseph and Benjamin. She figured in Dante's symbolic dream in Purgatory. Cf. *Purg.* 27.

Rahab (9). The harlot of Jericho whose aid to Joshua in his capture of the city (Hebrews 11) won her salvation.

Rebecca (32). Wife of Isaac, mother of Esau and Jacob.

Renouard (18). A gigantic warrior who fought with William of Orange against the Moors. He was a Saracen who had been converted to Christianity.

Richard of St. Victor (10). A twelfth-century theologian, pupil of Hugh of St. Victor.

Ripheus (20). Trojan warrior mentioned briefly in the *Aeneid* for his love of justice.

Robert Guiscard (18). Distinguished general in the wars of the Normans against the Saracens in southern Italy and Sicily in the eleventh century.

Roland (18). Nephew of Charlemagne; hero of the great medieval French epic, *Le Chanson de Roland.*

Romeo (6). Seneschal of Raymond Berengar, Count of Provence, in the early thirteenth century.

Romualdus (22). Founder of the Order of Reformed Benedictines.

Rudolph I of Hapsburg (8). Emperor from 1272-92. One of the emperors censured by Dante for neglect of Italy. Cf. *Purg.* 6-7.

Ruth (32). Heroine of the Book of Ruth, great-grandmother of David.

Sarah (32). Wife of Abraham.

Sardanapalus (15). King of Assyria, cited by Dante as an example of one living a life of luxury and depravity.

Scala, Bartolommeo della (17). Lord of Verona and one of Dante's patrons during his exile.

Scala, Can Grande della (17). Son of Bartolommeo. Dante placed his hopes in him as the future savior of Italy. He dedicated *Paradiso* to Can Grande and submitted the MS to him. Cf. *Inf.* 1, *Purg.* 20, 33.

Scipio (6). Roman general, victor in the Carthaginian campaign in 202 B.C. Given the title of "Africanus."

Sigier of Brabant (10). A professor at Paris who engaged in a violent debate with Thomas Aquinas over the teachings of Averroes.

Sixtus I, Bishop of Rome (27). A second-century exemplar of the virtuous early popes.

Solon (8). Famous judge in ancient Greece.

Sychaeus (9). Husband of Dido. When he was murdered in their homeland, Phoenicia, Dido escaped and founded the new colony of Carthage.

Tiberius. Cf. Caesar, Tiberius.

Titus, Emperor (6). The Roman commander who captured and destroyed Jerusalem in 70 A.D.

Tobit (4). Principal character in the Book of Tobit (in the Apocrypha) whose blindness was cured by the archangel Raphael.

Torquatus (6). A Roman leader of the fourth century B.C.

Trajan, Emperor (20). One of the best of all the Roman emperors; he reigned from 98-117 A.D.

Typhoeus (8). Monster overthrown by Jupiter and buried under Mt. Aetna.

Ubaldo, St. (11). He lived in a hermitage near Gubbio (in the vicinity of Assisi) before he became Bishop of Gubbio in the early twelfth century.

Ulysses (27). One of the Greek leaders in the Trojan War. He played a prominent role in the *Iliad* and was the central figure in the *Odyssey*. Cf. *Inf.* 26; *Purg.* 19.

Urban I (27). Bishop of Rome in the early third century who was martyred.

Veronica, St. (31). Lady whose veil bore the imprint of Christ's features. It was revered as one of the most precious of all holy relics.

Virgil (15, 17, 26). Roman poet, first century B.C., author of the *Aeneid*. He was called "master" by Dante and served as the poet's guide through Inferno and Purgatory.

Wenceslas IV, King of Bohemia (19). Contemporary of Dante who ruled from 1278-1305. Cf. *Purg.* 7.

William, Count of Orange (18). Hero of several *chansons de geste*, he fought against the Saracens.

William II, King of Sicily and Naples (20). Called "the Good," he ruled in the second half of the twelfth century.

Xerxes, King of Persia (8). The Persian king who led an invasion of Greece, c. 480 B.C. The war involved famous battles at Thermopole, Marathon, and Salamis.

REVIEW QUESTIONS AND STUDY PROJECTS

1. What scheme is employed to give *Paradiso* a structural pattern that parallels the plans of *Inferno* and *Purgatorio?*

2. What are the basic differences between the Ptolemaic astronomy and Copernican astronomy?

3. Do the spirits in Paradise have their permanent abodes in the planetary spheres where Dante meets them or in the Empyrean?

4. In what spheres are the spirits seen only as bright spots of light?

5. What is the astronomical peculiarity of the three lowest planets that marks them with "the taint of earth"?

6. Why are the spirits in those three lowest spheres held to enjoy degrees of blessedness inferior to those above?

7. Name the regions of Paradise in order, and specify the characteristics or vocations of the spirits encountered in each.

8. Specify the emblems formed by the lights in the several spheres and explain the significance of each.

9. Identify each of the following characters, designate his or her sphere, and report the substance of Dante's discourse with each: Cacciaguida, Cunizza, Justinian, Peter Damian, Piccarda Donati, St. Benedict, St. Bernard of Clairvaux, St. Bonaventura, St. Peter, and St. Thomas Aquinas.

10. Give an account of the life of Beatrice and of Dante's association with her.

11. What is the allegorical concept that Beatrice stands for in the *Comedy?*

12. Cite several puzzling subjects which Beatrice expounds for Dante in her role as guide and instructress.

13. What means does Dante employ to impress the reader with his personal adoration of Beatrice?

14. What types of sensations and emotions are introduced into Dante's heaven, and what types are excluded?

15. What type of passages has led some of Dante's detractors to accuse him of venting his spleen on persons and institutions against whom he bore a grudge?

16. Cite several contemporary political figures mentioned, and determine from their treatment what the author's views on national and international affairs were.

17. Cite several contemporary ecclesiastical figures and discuss the author's stand on Church politics.

18. Describe the Celestial Rose and indicate the arrangement of spirits there.

19. Paraphrase Dante's account of the Vision of God (the Beatific Vision).

20. Compare the use of similes in *Paradiso* with their use in *Inferno* and *Purgatorio:* that is, frequency, subjects, tone.

21. Give several examples of the employment of the obscure or indirect style in *Paradiso*. Consider the nature of the context of the passages, and explain what kind of appeal they held for Dante's more erudite contemporaries.

SELECTED BIBLIOGRAPHY

BRANDEIS, IRMA (ed.). *Discussions of the Divine Comedy.* Boston: D. C. Heath, 1961. Comments and essays on Dante by writers of various periods, such as Boccaccio, Petrarch, Voltaire, Coleridge, Croce, Etienne Gilson, Allen Tate.

————. *The Ladder of Vision, A Study of Dante's Comedy.* Garden City, N. Y.: Anchor Books, 1962. Topical essays on several aspects of the *Comedy.* For the study of *Paradiso,* chapters III, IV, and V are especially pertinent.

CHANDLER, S. BERNARD, and MOLINARO, J. A. (eds.). *The World of Dante. Six Studies in Language and Thought.* Toronto: University of Toronto Press, 1965. Essays by Glauco Cambon, John Freccero, Joseph A. Mazzeo, et al.

CIARDI, JOHN (trans. and ed.). *Dante Alighieri, The Paradiso.* Introduction by John Freccero. New York and Toronto: The New American Library, 1970. An excellent verse translation, with extensive and valuable notes.

114

Cosmo, Umberto. *A Handbook to Dante Studies,* translated by David Moore. Oxford: Basil Blackwell, 1950. New York: Barnes and Noble. Excellent source of information on the author's life and times and his early works as well as the *Comedy.*

Dinsmore, Charles A. *Aids to the Study of Dante.* Boston: Houghton Mifflin, 1903. Elaborate handbook information and valuable commentary.

Eliot, T. S. "Dante," *Selected Essays, 1917-1932.* New York: Harcourt Brace, 1932. Part II of this celebrated essay is devoted specifically to *Purgatorio* and *Paradiso.*

Freccero, John (ed.). *Dante, A Collection of Critical Essays.* Englewood Cliffs, N.J.: Prentice-Hall, 1965. A collection of articles treating various aspects of Dante studies by such writers as Erich Auerbach, T. S. Eliot, Charles S. Singleton, and Charles Williams.

Gilbert, Allan. *Dante and His Comedy.* New York: New York University Press, 1963. A valuable study of the *Comedy* that is organized topically, with discussions centered on numerous aspects of structure, style, themes, and problems.

Grandgent, C. H. (ed.). *La Divina Commedia di Dante Alighieri.* Boston, New York, et al.: D. C. Heath, 1933. The text is in Italian. The English introduction and notes have become indispensable for Dante scholarship.

Sayers, Dorothy L. "'. . . And Telling You a Story': a Note on *The Divine Comedy,*" *Essays Presented to Charles Williams.* London: Oxford University Press, 1947. An essay treating the story-telling techniques and the careful structural design of the *Comedy.*

Sayers, Dorothy L., and Reynolds, Barbara (trans. and eds.). *The Comedy of Dante Alighieri the Florentine: Cantica III, Paradise.* Baltimore: Penguin Books, 1962. Introduction, pp. 13-52, is detailed, perceptive, and eminently readable. The notes, diagrams, and appendices are elaborate and extremely valuable, especially for advanced students.

Sinclair, John D. (trans. and ed.). *The Divine Comedy of Dante Alighieri, Vol. III, Paradiso.* New York: Oxford University Press, 1961. A bilingual edition which offers an excellent literal prose translation. At the end of each canto the editor supplies brief factual notes plus an analytical-critical essay.

WILLIAMS, CHARLES. *The Figure of Beatrice.* London: Faber and Faber Ltd., 1943. A classic study of the life of Beatrice and her role in the works of Dante. Some of its interpretations are subject to controversy.

NOTES

NOTES

NOTES

NOTES

NOTES